Foolish
Words

"What we are doing is in the interest of everybody, bar possibly the consumer"

"I think there is a world market for maybe five computers"

"I'm not an egomaniac like a lot of people say. But I'm the world's best dancer, that's for sure"

"I declare this thing open—whatever it is"

Street hockey is great for kids. It's energetic, competitive and skilful. And best of all it keeps them off the street"

"We're going to turn this team around 360 degrees"

Caution: blade is extremely sharp. Keep out of children

"Are you Indian or Pakistani? I can never tell the difference between you chaps"

"Of all the things I've lost, it's my mind I miss the most"

"If you can't stand the heat in the dressing room, get out of the kitchen"

"Gaiety is the most outstanding feature of the Soviet Union"

Foolish Words

The most stupid words ever spoken

Laura Ward

PRC

Produced 2003 by
PRC Publishing Limited,
The Chrysalis Building
Bramley Road, London W10 6SP

An imprint of **Chrysalis** Books Group plc

This edition published 2003
Distributed in the U.S. and Canada by:
Sterling Publishing Co., Inc.
387 Park Avenue South
New York, NY 10016

ISBN 1 85648 698-2

Printed and bound in Malaysia

Contents

Introduction

"Don't mention the war!" screams Basil Fawlty in a classic
episode of the British television series *Fawlty Towers*, before
proceeding to do exactly that at each and every inopportune
moment to a group of German tourists. The episode is farce of the
highest order, and the lunacy works so well partly because it
conveys—as do all comedy classics—something of the essence of
what it is to be human. After all, we've all been there (admit it,
you have too). The phrase, once uttered, which leaves the speaker
frozen like a rabbit caught in the glare of the headlights. Or, to
quote no less an authority than Dan Quayle, former senator and
Vice-President of the United States: "Every once in a while, you
let a word or phrase out, and you want to catch it and bring it

back. You can't do that. It's gone, gone forever," he lamented, and with more justification than most. This, of course, has to be balanced against his claim to assembled reporters that, "public speaking is very easy." Speaking, I think we'd all concur, is not the problem here.

This book unashamedly eavesdrops on the verbal gaffes, goofs, boobs, blunders, flubs, *faux pas*, Freudian slips, call them what you will—there is no shortage of words for the practice in the English language, which denotes its ancient and worthy lineage—of our fellow unthinking or cerebrally-challenged Homo sapiens. It is a journey from the sublime to the ridiculous—and back again. The foolishness encapsulated embraces the full spectrum of daftness, from the "once spoken, never forgotten," nailing of colors to the ill-fated mast, to the out-of-synch lip dance—where the tongue is working faster than the brain—and to the butchering of syntax and mangling of metaphors. In addition to the outright verbal banana skins, a sense of (unjustifiable) smugness is to be gained through the plethora of unfortunate forecasts and other blasts from the past, which the passage of time and the benefit of hindsight have proven to be just so many empty words. "My, they were all so naïve back then," we laugh to ourselves, indulgently. Therein lies a lesson to one and all—always to hedge your bets.

The untoward utterances between these covers may issue from the mouths of those occupying the highest offices in the land, or simply convey the unguarded sayings of Joe Blow and the like. Businessmen, bureaucrats and bumbling lawyers are represented, as are celebrities, sports personalities, thespians or "luvvies," along with the muddled moments of radio and television presenters. A lack of joined-up thinking is a common thread, though space enough has been left for the more outrageous lapses of political correctness. "Give them enough rope, and they'll hang themselves," is the phrase that springs to mind; coupled with a healthy bit of sparring between the sexes.

I confess a particular fondness for laughably, planet-sized egos, in the manner of the Italian fascist dictator Mussolini: "This is the epitaph I want on my tomb: Here lies one of the most intelligent animals who ever appeared on the face of the earth." Ditto for shameless convictions of social superiority, or examples of overriding pretentiousness; these, too, have earned their respective places in the "foolishness" annals. Thus David Hasselhoff of *Baywatch* fame, with the claim, "There are many dying children out there whose last wish is to meet me," which could, of course, be taken the other way. Or the late Barbara Cartland, queen of romantic fiction: ". . . Of course they have, or I wouldn't be sitting here talking to someone like you," when asked whether class barriers in England were breaking down.

Many of the most memorably foolish lines come from our elders and betters—a.k.a. our political masters (and—though less often—mistresses), who are veritable sitting ducks for the hungry bird on the lookout for a juicy, if mangled, word worm.

(There, you see, it's catching, this mixing of metaphors.) Messrs George Bush Senior and Junior are masters of this art, scooping prizes for the "sentence going nowhere" and the "impenetrable bunkum" awards. Dubya is, in fact, a chip off ol' Poppy's block. (Bush Senior once admitted, "Fluency in English is something that I'm often not accused of," while Junior was dubbed, "the English patient," during his own presidential campaign.)

But there is a serious side to foolishness, too; those moments in history where ears are pricked, pens are poised or cameras rolling, and the words spoken are captured from the ether, ready to come back to haunt their owner. These are the misreadings and misjudgements of world-changing events which go down in the history books. For example, British Prime Minister Neville Chamberlain announcing the Munich Agreement, on 30 September 1938, as being, "symbolic of the desire of our two peoples (Britain and Germany) never to go to war with one another again." Or to go back much further in time: "I tell you that

Wellington is a bad general, that the English are bad troops, and that this affair is only a *déjeuner*," Napoleon is said to have cried on the morning of the Battle of Waterloo, 18 June 1815.

Lies, damned lies, though far from being "laugh out loud," humorous are similarly worthy of inclusion (viz. Nixon and the Watergate scandal, the Clinton/Lewinsky affair, or former MP Neil Hamilton and those brown-paper envelopes stuffed with cash he received from Harrods' boss Mohamed Al Fayed). Then there is the phrase that, unknown to its speaker, tells it like it really is—for example, Margaret Thatcher announcing royally, "We are a grandmother."

Staying with the "Royal We," as it were, Prince Philip has for a long time been working tirelessly to raise public awareness of the Art of Dentopology ("putting one's foot in one's mouth"). For decades now, his gaffes have been coming thick and fast, and the classics are unrivalled: "The bastards murdered half my family," he riposted in 1967, when asked whether he would consider a visit to Russia. As the Duke of Edinburgh himself has confessed: "As so very often happens, I discover that it would have been better to keep my trap shut." Quite so. The Queen, however, is not so proficient.

Some individuals have committed so many gaffes in the same vein that they have been fortunate enough to have their quips named after them. Take "Goldwynisms," the *bons mots* of movie mogul Samuel Goldwyn, who was notorious for his misuse and abuse of the language, or the sayings of the Reverend William Archibald Spooner, Anglican priest and Warden of New College, Oxford. The latter, though blessed with a sharp mind, had the habit of unintentionally transposing the sounds of different words, with some startling results: "Gentlemen, raise your glasses to the queer old dean." (He was, of course, toasting the reigning monarch, Queen Victoria.) Many spoonerish phrases of uncertain origin have consequently been attributed to the kindly and well-meaning old gentleman.

Similarly, American baseball legend "Yogi" Berra (who got his nickname long before Hanna Barbera's smarter-than-the-average bear) can claim to be one of the most quoted figures in the world of sport, and is credited with having invented the phrase, "It ain't over till it's over." Which raises a thorny issue—who is to say what is foolish? Berra's phrase, although stating the obvious, nonetheless contains a nugget of truth. Many other similarly gnome-like phrases have been included in this book, not in any spirit of maliciousness, but out of sheer glee at the huge variety of contortions into which the spoken word can be twisted with entertaining results.

And it's not just the spoken word—the written word has also earned its laurels. One of the richest sources is the age-old schoolroom blunder, or exam paper mistake. The ingenuity of many of these flights of fancy lifts the spirits and enlivens the imagination—after all, you couldn't make up: "A fort is a place to put men in, and a fortress a place to put women in," if you tried. A small number from a vast selection have therefore been included here, interspersed with a handful of offerings from those who "should know better"—in short, newspaper typos and gaffes from the "grown-ups."

The opportunity of including some famously foolish last words—or ominously prescient ones—was one too good to be passed up. "I am about to—or am I going to—die; either expression is used," was the brilliant dying phrase of the ever-punctilious French grammarian and Jesuit priest, Dominique Bouhours. Certain epitaphs and other engravings on aged tombstones are also included for merriment's sake.

In sum, this volume scrapes only the surface of the fount of foolishness, whose depths seem to plumb infinity. It is encouraging, then, to know that greater minds than ours have committed untoward utterances which make it seem as though our own daily gaffes and ghastly embarrassments are, in comparison, mild mishaps. So it's hoped this book will bring a smile to the face, and also bring reassurance to fellow dentopologists up and down the land. For myself, the "wig episode" (in fact, an anecdote passed on by a former colleague) still strikes a chord. It goes thus; all present are begged not to mention a certain individual's hairpiece, but it's no wonder that one person, inevitably, offers—while passing round the teapot— that particular individual, "a cup of wig." This is about my level of blunder. The joy of these foolish words is that others have erred with greater flair, imagination and overreaching ineptitude. But at least they have dared to put themselves on the line, while more cowardly folk have just kept it zipped.

After all, it is better to live and lapse, than never to live at all.

Laura Ward

May 2003

Rich & Famous—
celebrity gaffes and
royal rumpuses

Beyond its entertainment value, *Baywatch* has enriched and, in many cases, helped save lives. I'm looking forward to the opportunity to continue with a project which has had such a significance for so many.

David Hasselhoff, star of Baywatch

How else do you get on in this world except by marrying well?

Nigel Dempster, society chronicler, April 1977

You were playing your instruments weren't you? Or do you have tape-recorders under your seats?

Prince Philip, "congratulating" a school band on their performance in Cairns, Australia, 2002

I don't feel we did wrong in taking this great country away from them. There were great numbers of people who needed new land, and the Indians were selfishly trying to keep it for themselves.

John Wayne

They are my tits and if I wanna have them put on my back that is my own damn business.

Cher

I feel my best when I'm happy.

Winona Ryder

If you're a fifty pence piece in a pile of ten pence pieces, you have to shine so much brighter in order to be noticed.

Bono

It is true, Sir, that there has been some neglect; but I have taken care that the next coronation shall be regulated in the exactest manner possible.

Lord Effingham, Deputy Early Marshal, apologizing to King George I after his coronation had not gone to plan. The promise to rectify things next time around can hardly have filled King George with glee

Unless one is there, it's embarrassing. Like hearing the Lord's Prayer while playing canasta.

The (late) Queen Mother, speaking of the National Anthem

My main hope for myself is to be where I am.

Woody Harrelson

I can always judge people by the way they ring my doorbell.

Cynthia Payne, former London madam, October 1982

It looks as if it was put in by an Indian.

> *Prince Philip, pointing at an old-fashioned fuse box while on a tour of a factory near Edinburgh in 1999*

The things I know make sense.

> *Jade from the reality TV series* Big Brother

You can hardly tell where the computer models finish and the real dinosaurs begin.

> *Laura Dern, on the technical tricks employed in the film* Jurassic Park

I think the biggest disease the world suffers from in this day and age is the disease of people feeling unloved. I know that I can give love for a minute, for half an hour, for a day, for a month, but I can give. I am very happy to do that, I want to do that.

> *Diana, Princess of Wales*

To have your niece die in your arms is the greatest gift from God.

> *Celine Dion*

Are they going to chop off his head?

> *The young Princess Margaret, on the abrupt departure of "Uncle David"—who would have been crowned Edward VIII—following the 1936 Abdication Crisis*

The best thing to do with a degree is to forget it.

> *Prince Philip, at the University of Salford*

I have a responsibility to show that a young, married couple can still be happy
in our business.

> *Sonny Bono, of Sonny and Cher in 1965. (They split up some time later)*

Ich bin warm.

> *Sting, explaining to his audience at a German concert that he was feeling hot.*
> *To them, however, he was announcing, "I am gay"*

I don't know all the certain words to word it.

> *Vanilla Ice, on why he hired a ghostwriter for his autobiography*

I loved Jordan. He was one of the greatest athletes of our time.

> *Mariah Carey, on the death of the King of Jordan*

I feel that there could be no more suitable body or organization of men to
stretch forth the hand of friendship to the Germans than we ex-servicemen
who fought them and have now forgotten all about it and the Great War.

> *The Prince of Wales addressing a gathering of the British Legion in 1935.*
> *Edward abdicated a year later and left his brother George to deal*
> *with the Germans in World War II*

I believe there would be people alive today if there were a death penalty.

> *Nancy Reagan*

Well, I'm off to have a stubby.

> *Lord Snowdon, arriving in Australia amid rumors of divorce*

The only happy artist is a dead artist, because only then you can't change.

After I die, I'll probably come back as a paintbrush.

Sylvester Stallone

The number is less.

Prince Philip, querying a plaque at Amritsar in India, on which it said that 2,000 had died in the massacre (it was here, in 1919, that 379 Indians were shot by the British Army)

Manchester, that's not such a nice place.

Queen Elizabeth II on a visit to St Petersburg in 1994, during which a Russian student told her that she had been to England and had stayed in Manchester

Every city I go to is an opportunity to paint, whether it's Omaha or Hawaii.

Tony Bennett, singer

Fiction writing is great, you can make up almost anything.

Ivana Trump, on her first novel

I'll never get married again.

Elizabeth Taylor, in 1982

Elizabeth and I have been through too much to watch our marriage go up in flames. There is just too much love going for us ever to divorce.

Richard Burton, speaking amid rumors of troubles with his wife, Elizabeth Taylor, in 1974

You can't have been here that long, you haven't got a potbelly.

Prince Philip to a Briton residing in Hungary

Oh, I'm so sorry, I didn't recognize you without your crown.

Lady Diana Cooper, realizing at a party that the woman
she was talking to was Queen Elizabeth II

I have never been to Burma and I have never even seen the place. I cannot say I
am very sorry. I am not particularly fond of rain.

Prince Philip at the Burma Star Association Reunion

There is certainly more in the future now than back in 1964.

Roger Daltrey of The Who

I'm learning English at the moment. I can say "Big Ben," "Hello Rodney,"
"Tower Bridge" and "Loo."

Cher

Dontopedalogy is the science of opening your mouth and putting your foot in it,
a science which I have practiced for a good many years.

Prince Philip

My hairdresser calls me Beaujolais.

Victoria Beckham, referring to the British TV soap series Footballers' Wives,
which featured a female character called "Chardonnay"

I never see any home cooking – all I get is fancy stuff.

Prince Philip in 1962 (the remark was taken as a slight against
Buckingham Palace chefs, and later had to be qualified)

. . . sometimes like a grandfather clock, sometimes like an alarm clock, sometimes a cornucopian goddess, sometimes a curmudgeonly landlord, sometimes like the blossomiest blossom, sometimes a knot of seaweed, sometimes a storm, sometimes a cradle, sometimes the bees and the pollen, sometimes a dagger.

Actress Imogen Stubbs, on how she "feels as a mother," Daily Telegraph.
Sent in to the "Pseuds' Corner" column of Private Eye

Nothing really helps you face your own problems.

Agony Aunt Anna Raeburn, shooting herself in the foot when commenting on
the break-up of her marriage in 1974

You shouldn't stay here too long or you'll turn slitty-eyed.

Prince Philip, talking to British students in Beijing, China, during an official
visit in 1986. (Also reported as, "If you stay here much longer,
you'll all be slitty-eyed")

(A) Leper Colony.

Princess Diana describing the British royals

What is a Liberal Democrat?

Helen, on the TV series Big Brother

My husband is taking legal advice.

> *Lady Denning, wife of Britain's top judge, whose publisher was threatening to*
> *withdraw his latest book following libel threats in June 1982*

I can't deny the fact you like me. Right now, you like me.

> *Sally Field, gushing in her acceptance of the Oscar for Best Actress in 1984*
> *for the film* Places in the Heart

The British monarchical system is the highest pinnacle of achievement in the
ordering of human affairs and without doubt it is our destiny to protect and
nurture it and keep it as an example to the world.

> *Brigadier Richard Eason, head of the Australian pro-monarchist*
> *"British Brotherhood"*

There was never anyone called "Crap."

> *Jade on the TV series* Big Brother, *on being told by one of her housemates that*
> *the lavatory was invented by a man named Thomas Crapper*

I would not have been able to play this role had I not understood love with a
tremendous magnitude.

> *Gwyneth Paltrow, expressing her enormous gratitude to all concerned and*
> *sobbing uncontrollably as she accepted the Oscar for Best Actress in 1998, for*
> *her performance in* Shakespeare in Love

I've looked in the mirror every day for twenty years. It's the same face.

> *Claudia Schiffer*

No, I just look like him.

> *The words on the T-shirt worn by Prince Edward at the disastrous* It's A Royal Knockout *charity event at Alton Towers in 1987. The day left the Prince in a foul mood, his parting shot to the press photographers (having already kicked over a chair in front of the assembled reporters with a petulant "Right, that's it") was, "One of these days you people are going to have to learn some manners." It was a stupendous royal gaffe—and a gift to the assembled press corps*

I went in and said, "If I see one more gratuitous shot of a woman's body, I'm quitting . . ." I think the show should be emotional storylines, morals, real-life heroes. And that's what we're doing.

> *David Hasselhoff, explaining the new, highbrow angle in beach-babe TV series* Baywatch

Are you Indian or Pakistani? I can never tell the difference between you chaps.

> *Prince Philip at a Washington Embassy reception for Commonwealth members*

We'll be together forever. We are like twins.

> *Britt Ekland, of her new boyfriend Rod Stewart (in 1976 . . .)*

My body is in tumult . . . I would like to be . . . lying down and making love to everybody.

> *Roberto Benigni, the double Oscar winner of 1998 (for Best Actor and Best Foreign Film) in his acceptance speech—in broken English—for his film* Life is Beautiful. *He later added, "I am so happy, I want to wag my tail"*

When my Azzedine jacket from 1987 died, I wrapped it up in a box, attached a
note saying where it came from and took it to the Salvation Army. It was a big
loss.

Veronica Webb, actress

It's like swimming in undiluted sewage.

Prince Charles emerging from the surf at St Kilda Beach, near Melbourne.
The comment caused a storm in Australia (Charles deserved "a good thump
under the ear," according to one local mayor)

If it has got four legs and it is not a chair, if it has two wings and it flies but is
not an aeroplane, and if it swims and it is not a submarine, the Cantonese will
eat it.

Prince Philip commenting on Chinese eating habits
to a World Wildlife Fund conference in 1986

I want to take this opportunity to say how proud I am of my little brother, my
dear, sweet, talented brother. Just imagine what you could accomplish if you
tried celibacy.

Shirley Maclaine, presenting an Oscar to her (not amused)
brother Warren Beatty for Reds *in 1981*

Just as we can't blame people for their parents, we can't blame South America
for not having been members of the British Empire.

Prince Philip, speaking at the British and Latin American
Chambers of Commerce

You know, the Queen really rather likes me.

> *Koo Stark, Prince Andrew's girlfriend in February 1983*

Pretty amazing!

> *Diana's recollected reaction on meeting Prince Charles in a ploughed field in 1977, when asked in 1981 what her first impression had been*

You mean like a book?

> *Justin Timberlake when asked during a* Rolling Stone *interview what was the best thing he had read all year*

I'm confused. I thought Cambridge was in London. I knew Birmingham weren't in London.

> *The geographically-challenged Jade on the TV series* Big Brother

East Angular? That's abroad. Is there not a place called East Angular abroad? Every time people tell me they work in East Angular, I actually think they're talking about near Tunisia and places like that. Am I thick?

> *Jade on the TV series* Big Brother, *trying to make sense of the exact whereabouts of the English region of East Anglia (prompting the enquiry, "Jade, have you been taking stupid pills again?") She actually lived less than 15 miles from East Anglia*

Reichskanzler.

> *Prince Philip's welcome greeting to German leader Helmut Kohl at a trade fair. The last German chancellor to use the title was Hitler*

If I talk too much about things of which I have never claimed any special
knowledge, just contemplate the horrifying prospect if I were to get my teeth
into something even remotely familiar.

Prince Philip

I am a really big Elvis fan and I think the reason why we did the whole Elvis
thing is because, you know, he's from Vegas.

Britney Spears (Elvis was actually from Tupelo, Mississippi; but lived in
Memphis, Tennessee, a lot of his adult life)

I just want to thank everyone I met in my entire life.

Kim Basinger, during her Oscar acceptance speech, March 1998

If a cricketer, for instance, suddenly decided to go into a school and batter a lot
of people to death with a cricket bat, which he could do very easily, I mean,
are you going to ban cricket bats?

Prince Philip in 1996, amid calls to ban firearms after the Dunblane shootings

I don't wake up for less than $10,000 a day.

Linda Evangelista, supermodel

Superficiality and vulgarity, especially in women.

Nancy Reagan, owning up to her pet hates in December 1981

I really am a cat transformed into a woman.

Brigitte Bardot, quoted by Tony Crawley in, Bébé: The Films of Brigitte Bardot

Brian: What if she (Helen) has got an IQ of 25?

Helen: Actually, I'm only 23.

Exchange on the TV series Big Brother

Do you happen to know the name of the president of Russia, for instance? I
    don't think anyone's heard of him. He's just elected or appointed—I don't
    know. But he's a non-entity as far as the rest of the world is concerned. With
    us we just choose the son and the father. Somebody's got to do the job, why
    not do it that way?

Prince Philip

I like most of the places I've been to, but I've never really wanted to go to Japan,
    simply because I don't like eating fish, and I know that's very popular out
    there in Africa.

Britney Spears

For twenty years I was cornered and hounded like an animal. I didn't throw
    myself off my balcony only because I knew people would photograph me
    lying dead.

Brigitte Bardot (attrib.)

You can never be too rich or too thin.

Wallis Simpson

I declare this thing open—whatever it is.

Prince Philip, opening an annexe to Vancouver City Hall

Dig that crazy rhythm.

> *HRH Prince Charles trying—and failing conspicuously—to be cool as a DJ*
> *at a Prince's Trust-backed shelter*

I would not live forever, because we should not live forever, because if we were
  supposed to live forever, then we would live forever, but we cannot live
  forever, which is why I would not live forever.

> *Miss Alabama in the 1994 Miss USA contest. This was her answer to the*
> *question, '"If you could live forever, would you and why?"*

I'd rather be dead than singing *Satisfaction* when I'm 45.

> *Mick Jagger in 1970. Jagger was born in 1943, which made him 60 years old*
> *in 2003—yet those famous lips are still singing*

It's a beautiful park, but what a shame it's surrounded by all those nasty houses.

> *Queen Mary, opening a public park in Glasgow in the 1920s*

I would like to spank director Spike Jonze.

> *Meryl Streep, misreading a faxed acceptance speech*
> *at the 2003 Bafta Awards*

It's so bad being homeless in winter. They should buy a plane ticket and go
  somewhere hot like the Caribbean where they can eat free fish all day.

> *Lady Victoria Hervey, the so-called "It girl"*
> *(reportedly overheard remark)*

So, where's the Cannes Film Festival being held this year?

Christina Aguilera

That's all right, but you still haven't found out what makes the bath water
gargle when you pull the plug out.

Prince Philip to a scientist who was showing him around
the National Physical Laboratory

You can get much further with a kind word and a gun than you can with just
a kind word.

Al Capone, quoted in The Independent

Isn't Halle Berry the most beautiful woman? I have a film I'd like to be in her
with. I mean, I'd like to be with her in.

Ewan McGregor, actor, to an interviewer at the 2002 Golden Globe Awards

The problem with London is the tourists. They cause the congestion. If we
could just stop tourism we could stop the congestion.

Prince Philip, commenting on Mayor Ken Livingstone's introduction of the
Congestion Charge in central London in February 2003

Is the jelly cooked?

Helen, on the TV series Big Brother

As I said to the Queen, I can't stand name-droppers.

Globetrotting TV presenter, Alan Whicker

Do you know where my husband is?

>*Sarah Ferguson, Duchess of York, to the Mayoress of Maidenhead,*
>*after losing sight of Prince Andrew—from whom she was divorced in 1996—*
>*on their first official royal function together for four years.*

I suppose a knighthood is out of the question now?

>*Spike Milligan in a telegram to Prince Charles following his famous "little*
>*grovelling bastard" remark (he later received an honorary knighthood)*

I don't need the security of marriage. What I need is a romantic attachment.

>Playboy *boss Hugh Hefner, aged 75, who professed to having seven girlfriends*
>*(all blonde, all very young), on why he will never re-marry*

People usually say that after a fire it's the water damage that's the worst. We're
still trying to dry out Windsor Castle.

>*Prince Philip, to the grieving inhabitants of the Scottish town of Lockerbie, after*
>*Pan Am flight 103 had been brought down there on 21st December 1988, killing*
>*everyone on board as well as residents of the town*

I expect a thirty-year apprenticeship before I am king.

>*Prince Charles*

I know nothing about nothing.

>*Former Playmate and TV presenter Anna Nicole Smith,*
>*the $100 million widow*

We've never had a holiday. A week or two at Balmoral, or ten days at
Sandringham is the nearest we get.

Princess Anne

I would like to be an archaeologist.

Mike Tyson, on his career options beyond the world of boxing

Aren't most of you descended from pirates?

Prince Philip, querying the ancestral origins of a wealthy Cayman Islander

God! There are nine of us in here . . . It does not seem to be as many as at the
start.

Helen, on the TV series Big Brother. *The idea of the show
is to evict one contestant a week*

It's a pleasant change to be in a country that isn't ruled by its people.

Prince Philip to Alfredo Stroessner, the Paraguayan dictator

I was naive in my youth.

*Charlotte Church, British classical singer, aged sixteen—
and reflecting on her "early" years*

I will feel equality has arrived when we can elect to office women who are as
incompetent as some of the men who are already there.

Maureen Reagan, daughter of the then President Reagan, in 1982

Sometimes as a bit of a twit.

Prince Charles, on being asked by David Frost how he would describe himself

What are they for?

Weakest Link TV presenter Anne Robinson on the Welsh nation, while condemning its inhabitants to Room 101—a place where guests shut away their pet hates—on the BBC2 program of the same name. The remark, which was widely reported, caused a furore in the media and proved that she can be consistently offensive, whichever program she appears on

So you're responsible for the kind of crap Channel Four produces.

Prince Philip, on being introduced to the chairman of the Channel Four television network

I resign in Florida.

Backstreet Boys' singer Nick Carter. The comment fooled the interviewer—and Carter's fellow band members—into thinking he was leaving the group

Deaf? If you are near there, no wonder you are deaf.

Prince Philip to young, deaf people in Cardiff in 1999, referring to a nearby school's welcoming steel band

Smoking kills. If you're killed, you've lost a very important part of your life.

Brooke Shields, offering up her nugget of truth during a national No Smoking campaign in the US

(Wonderful) to be on terracotta again.

> *Laura Corrigan, announcing her pleasure at being back on* terra firma
> *after disembarking from the yacht on which she had been cruising*

Oh, here comes Mel Blanc, the voice of Bugs Bunny and Jimmy Smits!

> *Roger Ebert, announcing the arrival of Mel Blanc and Jimmy Smits*
> *at the Academy Awards ceremony*

I've learned not to put things in my mouth that are bad for me.

> *Monica Lewinski on CNN's* Larry King Live. *They were discussing her*
> *weight loss through the Jenny Craig program. Her phrasing, it seems,*
> *was perfectly innocent . . .*

Prince Philip: Why are you dressed like that?

Dr Allende: Because my party is poor, and they advised me not to hire evening dress.

Prince Philip: If they told you to wear a bathing costume, I suppose you'd come dressed in one?

> *Prince Philip—in white tie evening dress—challenging Dr Salvador Allende,*
> *President of the Chilean Senate, on his lounge suit attire at a State banquet*

I'm practically unprepared.

> *Greer Garson, Hollywood legend, accepting the Oscar for Best Actress for her*
> *role in* Mrs Miniver—*despite being "unprepared," her speech went on for some*
> *seven minutes (but seemed more like 90, according to those who heard it)*

I know who I am. No one else knows who I am. If I was a giraffe and somebody
said I was a snake, I'd think, "No, actually I am a giraffe."

Richard Gere. The utterance won the actor the Plain English Campaign's 2002
award for a "truly baffling quote"

Where the hell is Australia anyway?

Britney Spears

They're self-indulged with themselves.

Helen, on the TV series Big Brother

If you travel as much as we do, you appreciate how much more comfortable
aircraft have become. Unless you travel in something called economy class,
which sounds ghastly.

Prince Philip, during the Royal Jubilee tour in 2002

The band never actually split up—we just stopped speaking to each other and
went our own separate ways.

Boy George, talking about Culture Club on BBC Radio 2

Cystitis is a living death, it really is. Nobody ever talks about it, but if I was
faced with a choice between having my arms removed and getting cystitis,
I'd wave goodbye to my arms quite happily.

Louise Wener of rock band Sleeper, in Q *magazine*

Well, naturally it is quite daunting, but I hope it won't be too difficult, and with Prince Charles beside me I can't go wrong.

Lady Diana Spencer, speaking in February 1981 (she had been asked how she would cope with her role as royal consort)

You know, British women can't cook. They are very good at decorating food and making it attractive. But they have an inability to cook.

Prince Philip, addressing his (predominantly female) audience when invited to attend the Scottish Rural Women's Institute Display in 1966

Changing someone's life is not the best, it is not wanting to change the other life. It is being who you are that changes another's life. Do you understand?

Juliette Binoche, French actress

I love blinking, I do!

Helen, on the TV series Big Brother

Who is Llewellyn?

Prince Charles, querying the name on a banner just before his investiture in 1969 at Caernarfon, Wales (the Welsh Nationalist demonstrator holding it replied, "Llewellyn was the last Welsh Prince of Wales")

Who is this Hitler, spoiling everything?

Princess Margaret, in 1939

In an action film you act in the action. If it's a dramatic film you act in the drama.

Jean-Claude Van Damme, action hero, explaining the actor's craft

Are you still throwing spears at other tribes?

Prince Philip to Ivan Brim, Djabugay Elder at Tjapukai Aboriginal Park, during a royal visit to Australia, 2002

It's too bad you sent your royal family to the guillotine, isn't it?

Prince Philip to a visiting French minister of the interior

I loved making *Rising Sun*. I got into the psychology of why she liked to get strangled and tied up in plastic bags. It has to do with low self-esteem.

Tatjana Patitz on her role in the film Rising Sun

Ghastly.

Prince Philip, commenting on Beijing, China, during an official visit in 1986. The trip produced a litany of similar gaffes

They don't do that on the Thames though, do they?

Jade on the TV series Big Brother, *after fellow housemate Spencer had been explaining about Venetian gondolas*

I know a lot of women who use men, but the world is not perfect. Fifty years ago there was Hitler; now there are bitches everywhere.

Actress, Julie Delpy

I think *Baywatch* is such a hit here (the UK) because of the weather.

> *Actress Gena Lee Nolin (nothing to do with the bronzed beach-babes, then)*

I get to go to a lot of famous places, like Canada.

> *Britney Spears on the good bits of being famous*

Anyone who makes fun out of *Baywatch* is doing it out of ignorance.

> *David Hasselhoff,* Baywatch *actor and later to become Executive Producer*

I'm the Hiroshima of love.

> *Sylvester Stallone*

(*Dances With Wolves*) is a bonding film for all. You could put it anywhere in history—the Berlin Wall, Kuwait.

> *Kevin Costner*

I've always been the one to push and shove and say, "Sorry, that's it darlin', it's all over, goodbye. Take twenty Valium and have a stomach pump and that's the end of it."

> *Rod Stewart, incurable romantic*

Announcement: This is Big Brother. A meteorite has landed in the garden. You have two minutes to get dressed.

Helen: Dressed? What, as in clothes?

> *Snippet from the TV series* Big Brother

The monarchy system adds gaiety to politics.

Prince Philip

The monarchy exists not for its own benefit, but for that of the country. If you don't want us, then let's end it on amicable terms and not have a row about it. We don't come here for our health. We can think of better ways of enjoying ourselves.

Prince Philip, during a royal visit to Ottawa in Canada in 1969

I think it is a perfectly valid system for producing a head of state. It's been very successful for 1,000 years. It's had its ups and downs, undoubtedly.

Prince Philip, on the monarchy

It's not that I dislike many people. It's just that I don't like many people.

Bryant Gumbel, TV newscaster

Charity is taking an ugly girl to lunch.

Warren Beatty

I think a man can have two, maybe three affairs, while he is married. But three is the absolute maximum. After that, you're cheating.

Yves Montand, French actor who hasn't read his ten commandments properly

I act from my crotch. That's where my force is.

Jeremy Irons, English actor

I was asked to come to Chicago because Chicago is one of our fifty-two states.

Raquel Welch, speaking on Larry King Live

A few years ago everybody was saying, "We must have more leisure, everybody's working too much." Now that everybody's got more leisure, they're complaining they're unemployed. People don't seem to be able to make up their minds what they want, do they?

Prince Philip, on being asked his thoughts on unemployment on The Jimmy Young Show *in 1981—a time when Britain was in a severe recession*

Everywhere I went, my cleavage followed. But I learned I am not my cleavage.

Carole Mallory, model (attrib.)

It's a good way to get rid of a few nuts, you know, you gotta look at it that way.

Ted Turner, TV mogul, looking on the bright side of the Heaven's Gate Cult mass suicide

God had to create disco music so that I could be born and be successful.

Donna Summer, singer

There aren't enough men to go around . . . Every time there's a plane accident, it's one hundred men dead . . . and I literally think, "Why couldn't some women have been on that flight?"

Helen Gurley Brown, Cosmopolitan *editor and author of* Sex And the Single Girl

Bloody silly fool!

> *Prince Philip in 1997, referring to a Cambridge University*
> *car park attendant who failed to recognize him.*

It seemed that my wife Shirley was always pregnant until we found out what
was causing it.

> *Pat Boone, singer, explaining why his wife hadn't*
> *accompanied him on trips previously*

People are dressing up more now because the idea of war hangs heavy in the
air . . . it is something that makes you think that, "I'd better do the best I can."

> *Joey Arias, New York drag chanteuse and long-time clubber,*
> *quoted in gay lifestyle magazine* Boyz

There are many dying children out there whose last wish is to meet me.

> *David Hasselhoff*

Aren't there any male supervisors? This is a nanny city.

> *Prince Philip in San Francisco, on meeting five city officials—*
> *all of whom were female*

Playboy isn't like the downscale, male bonding, beer-swilling phenomenon that
is being promoted now [by some men's magazines]. My whole notion was the
romantic connection between male and female.

> *Hugh Hefner*

At the risk of sounding pompous, I guess I would align it (playing with Tin
Machine in 1991) with deconstructionism. The point made by the French in
the Sixties that we are working our way towards a society that is deeply
involved with hybridization and contradictory information almost to the point
where contradiction simply ceases to exist . . .

David Bowie, taking the risk he refers to—and running all the way with it

If you have intercourse you run the risk of dying and the ramifications of death
are final.

Cyndi Lauper, singer

You are a woman, aren't you?

Prince Philip in Kenya in 1984, after accepting a small gift
from an indigenous woman

It sounds vain, but I could probably make a difference for almost everyone I ever
met if I chose to involve myself with them either professionally or personally.

Kevin Costner

I rather doubt whether anyone has ever been genuinely shocked by anything I
have said.

Prince Philip

I don't like telling clients [her hairdressing customers] that I teach dancing
because they might think I'm being big-headed.

Helen, on the TV series Big Brother.

[The movie *Amazon*] takes place in the Amazon and what you realize is that this man has to make major choices, and he makes major mistakes instead of the right things, and through his mistakes he learns a lot of soulful things, and he actually corrects his inner life, which, of course, helps enhance his outer life, and through the whole process we learn about how sad it is that we have something called the Amazon Forest and we're destroying it, and yet I say as an American-Canadian actress, it's sad what we're doing to [forests] in the Amazon.

Rae Dawn Chong, actress, quoted in Spy *magazine*

I'm still friends with all my ex's, apart from my husbands.

Cher

If you have a sense of duty, and I like to think I have, service means that you give yourself to people, particularly if they want you, and sometimes if they don't.

Prince Charles, commenting on the Prince of Wales' motto, "Ich Dien" (I Serve)

I'm the artist formally known as Beck. I have a genius wig. When I put that wig on, then the true genius emerges. I don't have enough hair to be a genius. I think you have to have hair going everywhere.

Beck

It can open doors. When I think about those who don't get the opportunity . . . I wrestle with that a bit.

Brad Pitt, on the advantage of being drop-dead handsome

If you gave a seven-year-old a brush and paints he'd produce something like
that.

> *Prince Philip in the Sudan, after viewing some of the paintings*
> *housed in the country's ethnic museum*

I love seeing all my Mexican fans from the north

> *Britney Spears, speaking on television in New York*

There's this idea that if you take your clothes off, somehow you must have loose
morals. There's still a negative attitude in our society towards women who
use a strength that's inherent—their femininity—in any way that might be
considered seductive.

> *Demi Moore*

I now complete the process of helping my father to expose himself.

> *Prince Charles, unveiling a bust of Prince Philip at the*
> *Royal Thames Yacht Club*

People have written and said when they've gone to a doctor's office to hear
about whether a tumor is benign or malignant, they've called upon Scully's
strength. It's kind of miraculous.

> *Gillian Anderson, of X-Files fame*

I discovered I scream the same way whether I'm about to be devoured by a
Great White or if a piece of seaweed touches my foot.

> *Axel Rose*

My dream role would probably be a psycho killer, because the whole thing I
love about movies is that you get to do things you could never do in real life,
and that would be my way of vicariously experiencing being a psycho killer.
Also, it's incredibly romantic.

Actress Christina Ricci

I'm king of the world!

James Cameron, crowing his acceptance of the Oscar for Best Director for
Titanic in 1998 (then he asked for a minute's silence, "in remembrance of the
1,500 men, women and children who died when the great ship went down,"
after which he shattered the pseudo-solemnity by screaming,
"Now, let's party till dawn!")

I sometimes think I was born to live up to my name. How could I be anything
else but what I am, having been named Madonna? I would either have ended
up a nun or this.

Madonna

The thing I might do best is be a long-distance lorry driver.

Princess Anne

Yes, I'm a virgin, and I do want to try to have sex until I'm married.

Britney Spears, in a Freudian slip on MTV

Sure I love Liam—but not as much as I love Pot Noodles.

Noel Gallagher of rock band Oasis

I probably sound Welsh on the telly.

Helen, from Wales, on the TV series Big Brother

The bastards murdered half my family.

Prince Philip, in a room full of press agents, commenting on the Russians in 1967. He had been asked whether he would consider a visit there

I wish people could achieve what they think would bring them happiness in order for them to realize that that's not what happiness really is.

Singer, Alanis Morissette

I am just too much.

Bette Davis, Hollywood legend

Death would be a beautiful place if it looks like Brad Pitt.

Carmen Electra, actress

Writing a book about Anne? Whatever for?

Prince Andrew, in a touching display of brotherly support, upon learning of just such a project

How do you keep the natives off the booze long enough to get them to pass the test?

Prince Philip, to a driving instructor in Scotland

It was not my class of people. There was not a producer, a press agent, a director, an actor.

> *Zsa Zsa Gabor, complaining about the make-up of the jury which convicted her of slapping a Beverly Hills police officer (the latter had halted her on a traffic violation)*

If I'm deciding on whom I want to live with for fifty years—well, that's the last decision on which I would want my head to be ruled by my heart.

> *Prince Charles in 1972*

Of all the things I've lost, it's my mind I miss the most.

> *Ozzy Ozbourne*

You managed not to get eaten, then.

> *Prince Philip, to a student who had been trekking in Papua New Guinea in 1998, and thereby suggesting that Papuan tribes people are still cannibals*

What's in kidney beans?

> *Helen, on the TV series* Big Brother

It's funny the way most people love the dead. Once you are dead, you are made for life.

> *Jimi Hendrix*

History—
and the beauty of 20/20 hindsight

To assert that the earth revolves around the sun is as erroneous [as] to claim that Jesus was not born of a virgin.

Cardinal Belleramine

Pish! A woman might piss it out.

Lord Mayor of London, on being told in the small hours of the morning of 13 September 1666 of a blaze in Pudding Lane. The Great Fire of London ensued

I do not think we shall hear much more of the general strike in our life.

Ramsay Macdonald, The Observer *"Sayings of the Week," May 1926*

Lord Uxbridge: I've lost my leg, by God!
Wellington: By God, sir, so you have!

Exchange at the Battle of Waterloo, 18 June 1815

I wouldn't believe Hitler was dead even if he told me so himself.

The Führer's Central Bank Governor, May 1945

There cannot always be fresh fields of conquest by the knife . . . That we have already, if not quite, reached these final limits, there can be little question. The abdomen, the chest, and the brain will be forever shut from the intrusion of the wise and humane surgeon.

> *Sir John Eric Erichsen, British surgeon (later appointed*
> *Surgeon Extraordinary to Queen Victoria) in 1873*

I hope that what I have said today will at least make television, radio and the press first recognize the great responsibility they have to report all the news and, second, recognize that they have a right and a responsibility, if they're against a candidate, to give him the shaft, but also recognize if they give him the shaft, put one lonely reporter on the campaign who will report what the candidate says now and then. Thank you gentlemen, and good day.

> *Richard Nixon bidding farewell to the press after his failed bid for the*
> *governorship of California in November 1962.*
> *("You won't have Nixon to kick around any more, gentlemen.*
> *This is my last press conference")*

Merde!

> *The famous (excretory) exclamation from Major General Pierre Cambronne,*
> *Napoleon's great military leader, moments before his capture at the Battle of*
> *Waterloo, 1815. (It became known as "le mot de Cambronne" (the word of*
> *Cambronne)*

I was an expert on migration problems.

> *Adolf Eichmann, January 1961*

I still believe I have a mission to carry out to the end, and I intend to carry it out to the end without giving up my throne. I'm convinced the monarchy in Iran will last longer than your regimes.

The (then) Shah of Iran in October 1973

Aujourd'hui, rien (today, nothing).

Diary entry from Louis XVI, King of France, on 14 July 1789—the day the Bastille was stormed

Germans who wish to use firearms should join the SS or the SA—ordinary citizens don't need guns, as their having guns doesn't serve the State.

Heinrich Himmler

Without censorship, things can get terribly confused in the public mind.

General William Westmoreland, during the war in Vietnam

I have been over into the future, and it works.

Lincoln Steffens, US journalist, on his return from a visit to Soviet Russia in 1919

The world then to an end shall come
In Eighteen Hundred and Eighty-One.

"Mother" Shipton (one of many erroneous predictions made by the "wise" old woman Shipton)

I do not know how many we shot . . . It all started when hordes of natives surrounded the police station. If they do these things they must learn their lesson the hard way.

Colonel Pienaar, Area Police Commander, speaking after the Sharpeville massacre in South Africa, March 1960

I do not believe in the probability of anything very much worse than mustard gas being produced.

Professor J.B.S. Haldane, 1937

The best defense against the atom bomb is not to be there when it goes off.

The British Army Journal, *February 1949*

The US must be willing to continue bombing until every work of man in North Vietnam is gone.

General Curtis Le May, October 1968

I will not resign. I declare my will to resist by every means, even at the cost of my life.

Salvador Allende, Chilean President, in September 1973. Such dogged resistance did indeed cost him his life when his government was overthrown in a violent, military coup

I have often said to myself that the history of South Africa is the one true and great romance of modern history.

General Smuts, May 1917

There seems to be something wrong with our bloody ships today.

> *Admiral Sir David Beatty's comment on 31 May 1916, following the sinking of*
> *British ships (including the* Queen Mary, *with the loss of 1,266 men) by the*
> *German fleet in the Battle of Jutland during World War I*

Who will rob me of this turbulent priest?

> *King Henry II of England, while in Caen, Normandy, on hearing*
> *that Archbishop Thomas Becket was continuing to oppose the royal will.*
> *It was a rhetorical statement, but one that the king would live to regret—*
> *four of his knights took him at his royal word and murdered Becket in*
> *Canterbury Cathedral*

One death is a tragedy; a million deaths is a statistic.

> *Josef Stalin (attrib.)*

Earlier a woman apparently called the BBC and said there's going to be a
hurricane . . . well, don't worry, there isn't. But there will be some strong
winds in Spain and across to France.

> *BBC weatherman Michael Fish, predicting a quiet night for the South*
> *of England on 15 October 1987 (the "Great Storm" that battered Southern*
> *England that night was the worst in 300 years, killing 18 people and flattening*
> *15 million trees)*

Writing about the Nixon Administration is about as exciting as covering the
Prudential Life Assurance Company.

> *Art Buchwald, July 1970*

When the Paris Exhibition closes, electric light will close with it and no more will be heard of it.

Professor Erasmus Wilson of Oxford University, 1878

Much of the trouble in Russia, politics apart, is due, I believe, to the fact that Russia is not a games-playing nation.

W.W. Wakefield, March 1928

This noblesse will ruin us.

Marie Antoinette—predicting things correctly, as it turned out

If the British attack our cities we will simply erase theirs. The hour will come when one of us will break up, and it won't be Nazi Germany.

Adolf Hitler, September 1940

Drill for oil? You mean drill into the ground to try and find oil? You're crazy.

Workers whom Edwin L. Drake tried to enlist to his project to drill for oil in 1859

To save the town, it became necessary to destroy it.

US officer, speaking in 1968 of an "incident" in the Vietnam War

Britain will not be involved in a European war this year, or next year either.

Front-page headline in British newspaper the Daily Express *on 30 September 1938 (headlines with the gist of, "There will be no European war" appeared several times in that paper between that date and August 1939, though not on the front page)*

In my opinion, the attempt to build up a Communist Republic on the lines of strongly-centralized State Communism, under the iron rule of the dictatorship of a party, is ending in failure.

Prince Kropotkin, The Observer *"Sayings of the Week", July 1920*

Let them eat cake.

Marie Antoinette—she meant "brioche," a sugary type of bread, but the comment nonetheless displayed her appalling ignorance of the famine and poverty then ravaging France, and further incited the mob against the royal pair

I put before the whole House my own views with appalling frankness . . . Suppose I had gone to the country and said that Germany was rearming, and that we must rearm, does anybody think that this pacific democracy would have rallied to that cry at that moment? I cannot think of anything that would have made the loss of the election from my point of view more uncertain.

British Prime Minister Stanley Baldwin to the House of Commons on 12 November 1936. (Winston Churchill later commented, "That a Prime Minister should avow that he had not done his duty in regard to national safety because he was afraid of losing the election was an incident without parallel in our Parliamentary history.") From Sayings of the Century, *by Nigel Rees*

I tell you that Wellington is a bad general, that the English are bad troops, and that this affair is only a *déjeuner.*

Attributed to Napoleon I on the morning of Waterloo, 18 June 1815

The most significant fact of modern history is that America speaks English.

Ludwig von Bismarck

Gaiety is the most outstanding feature of the Soviet Union.

Josef Stalin, November 1935

All those who are not racially pure are mere chaff.

Adolf Hitler, in Mein Kampf

I don't see much future for the Americans . . . Everything about the behavior of
American Society reveals that it's half-Judaized, and the other half negrified.
How can one expect a state like that to hold together?

Adolf Hitler, quoted in Hitler's Table Talk *(1953)*

What will she call herself? Queen of England, of course. And Empress of India,
the whole bag of tricks.

The never-to-be-crowned Edward VIII speaking of his consort, Wallis Simpson

After the war, there will be a revolution in the United States, and presumably
elsewhere, coming at a time of profound economic dislocation.

Leon Trotsky, in 1940

I'm not interested in a third party. I do not believe it has any future.

Shirley Williams, Labour politician speaking in 1980.
In 1981 she left Labour to form a fourth party, the Social Democratic Party, and
in 2001 was elected leader of the Liberal Democrats in the House of Lords

My good friends, this is the second time in our history that there has come back
from Germany to Downing Street peace with honor. I believe it is peace for
our time. Go home and get a nice, quiet sleep.

Neville Chamberlain, British Prime Minister, speaking at
10 Downing Street on the night of 30 September 1938,
following his return from a second visit to the German Chancellor,
Adolf Hitler, during which the Munich Agreement was signed

We have stopped losing the war in Vietnam.

Robert McNamara, US Defense Secretary, The Observer
"Sayings of the Week," December 1965

Mind you, people are never very receptive to innovation. Electric light will never
take the place of gas.

Werner Von Siemens, engineer and inventor, 1890.
He went on to found the multi-national Siemens corporation

The whole nation loves him, because it feels safe in his hands, like a child in the
arms of his mother.

Dr Joseph Goebbels, speaking of the German Chancellor,
Adolf Hilter, in 1934

God himself could not sink this ship.

Deckhand on the Titanic, which sank on the night of 14 April 1912,
on her maiden voyage

(A) bigger bang for a buck.

Comment by US secretary for defense, Charles E. Wilson, following the testing
of a new H-bomb at the Bikini atoll

I can't say I was ever lost, but I was bewildered once, for three days.

Daniel Boone, US pioneer (1734–1820)

We are winning international respect.

Adolf Hitler, The Observer "Sayings of the Week," 21 January 1934

A third-rate burglary attempt not worthy of further White House comment.

Ron Ziegler, White House press spokesman, on the
Watergate break-in, June 1972

The situation is splendid. God willing, we are going forward to great and
victorious days.

Kaiser Wilhelm, June 1918

The energy produced by the breaking down of the atom is a very poor kind of
thing. Anyone who looks for a source of power in the transformation of the
atom is talking moonshine.

Lord Ernest Rutherford, after splitting the atom, September 1933

We are all satisfied in South Africa now.

General Jan Smuts, The Observer "Sayings of the Week," December 1926

It was very successful, but it fell on the wrong planet.

> *Comment attributed to the German rocket engineer Werner von Braun,*
> *referring to the first V2 rocket (which he designed)*
> *to hit London during World War II*

Being a lady war correspondent is like being a lady wrestler—you can be one of them at a time, but not both simultaneously.

> *Dickey Chapelle, speaking at Danang, 2 November 1965.*
> *(Ms Chapelle was killed in action the following day)*

We shall never make war except for peace.

> *William McKinley, speech at El Paso, Texas, 6 May 1901*

That the king can do no wrong, is a necessary and fundamental principle of the English constitution.

> *Sir William Blackstone,* Commentaries on the Laws of England *(1765–9)*

I don't think there'll be war. The Führer doesn't want his new buildings bombed.

> *Unity Mitford, Adolf Hitler's English "companion," in 1938*

You English, are mad, mad, mad as March hares. What has come over you that you are so completely given over to suspicions quite unworthy of a great nation? What more can I do than I have done?

> *Kaiser Wilhelm in an interview with the* London Daily Telegraph,
> *28 October 1908*

War is a biological necessity of the first importance.

Friedrich von Bernhardt, 1911

We are not interested in the possibilities of defeat. They do not exist.

Queen Victoria, speaking of the Boer War, during which
British forces paid a heavy price

We shall reach the helm within five years.

Sir Oswald Mosley, The Observer "Sayings of the Week," January 1938

You will give England the most certain death stroke . . . We shall succeed in our enterprises . . . The fates are with us.

Napoleon, rallying his troops before the Battle of Waterloo, 1815

I cannot conceive of any condition which would cause a ship to founder. I cannot conceive of any vital disaster happening to a vessel. Modern shipbuilding has gone beyond that.

E.J. Smith, of the White Star Line, future captain of the Titanic

The British Army should be a projectile to be fired by the British Navy.

Lord Grey, 1862–1933

It's only a toy.

Gardiner Greene Hubbard, co-founder of the National Geographic Society and
inventor Alexander Graham Bell's future father-in-law, upon seeing Bell's
newfangled "telephone" in 1876

This morning I had another talk with the German Chancellor, Herr Hitler, and
here is the paper which bears his name upon it as well as mine . . . "We regard
the agreement signed last night, and the Anglo-German Naval Agreement, as
symbolic of the desire of our two peoples never to go to war with one another
again."

Prime Minister, Neville Chamberlain, speaking to reporters at Heston Airport,
30 September 1938, on his return from a second visit to Hitler,
during which the Munich Agreement was signed

War is the highest expression of the racial will to life.

Erich Ludendorff, in Meine Kriegserinnerungen, *1919*

I cannot see any nation or combination of nations producing the money
necessary to put up a satellite in outer space or to circumnavigate the moon.

Sir Richard Woolley, Astronomer Royal, in 1957 (or, as he put it
on another occasion, "space travel is utter bilge")

Remember, the German people are the chosen of God. On me, the German
Emperor, the spirit of God has descended. I am His sword, His weapon, and
His vice-regent.

Kaiser Wilhelm, 4 August 1914

By the end of 1991, it is not unreasonable to suppose, motoring will become an
occupation indulged in by the super-rich, just as it was in the early 1920s.

Lord Tanlaw, May 1977

POLITICS: Scotland to have total independence by 1985. The Irish problem to be solved in a close confederation between the United Kingdom, Ulster and Eire, with Eire joining the Commonwealth.

INTERNATIONAL SCENE: A United States of Europe by 1985, with one member—possibly France—expelled. Teddy Kennedy to be US President 1980–4. Richard Nixon to make a political comeback.

> *Predictions for the 1980s by* The Sun *newspaper's astrologer*
> *Roger Elliot in November 1979*

I feel very proud, even though they didn't elect me, to be president of the Argentines.

> *General Galtieri, 1982*

I often think how much easier the world would have been to manage if Herr Hitler and Signor Mussolini had been to Oxford.

> *Lord Halifax, November 1937*

I don't believe in black majority rule in Rhodesia . . . not in a thousand years.

> *Ian Smith, March 1976*

Everything that can be invented has been invented.

> *Charles H Duell, Commissioner of the US Office of Patents, 1899 (he was*
> *arguing for the abolition of the very office he occupied under*
> *President McKinley)*

It is quite clear to me that the Tory Party will get rid of Mrs Thatcher in about three years' time.

> *Sir Harold Wilson, former Labour Prime Minister,*
> *speaking in 1980, a year after she was elected.*
> *Thatcher would go on to win three general elections*

...this monkey mythology of Darwin is the cause of permissiveness, promiscuity, prophylactics, perversions, pregnancies, abortions, pornotherapy, pollution, poisoning and proliferation of crimes of all types.

> *Judge Braswell Dean*

I have determined that there is no market for talking pictures.

> *Thomas Edison, in 1926*

The Americans have need of the telephone, but we do not. We have plenty of messenger boys.

> *Sir William Preece*

What can be more palpably absurd and ridiculous than the prospect held out of locomotives travelling twice as fast as stage coaches!

> *Comment in* Quarterly Review, *March 1825*

Do not bother to sell your gas shares. The electric light has no future.

> *Professor John Henry Pepper on Thomas Edison's*
> *electric light invention*

Before man reaches the moon your mail will be delivered within hours from New York to Australia by guided missiles. We stand on the threshold of rocket mail.

> *Arthur Summerfield, US Postmaster General under*
> *President Eisenhower, in 1959*

It is impossible to transmit speech electrically. The "telephone" is as mythical as the unicorn.

> *Professor Johann Christian Poggendorrf, German physicist and chemist, 1860*

Nothing is gained by exaggerating the possibilities of tomorrow. We need not worry about the consequences of breaking up the atom.

> *Floyd W. Parsons, engineer, in the* Saturday Evening Post, *1931*

Aerial flight is one of that class of problems with which man cannot cope.

> *Simon Newcomb, US astronomer, 1903*

Although it is interesting as an interesting novelty, the telephone has no commercial application.

> *John Pierpoint Morgan (1837–1913) to Alexander Graham Bell*

Where a calculator on the ENIAC is equipped with 18,000 vacuum tubes and weighs 30 tons, computers in the future may have only 1,000 vacuum tubes and weigh only 1.5 tons.

> *Extract from the journal* Popular Mechanics, *March 1949*

X-rays will prove to be a hoax.

Lord Kelvin, Victorian physicist and President of the Royal Society, c.1896

...generations will pass before man ever lands on the Moon.

Sir Harold Spencer Jones in the New Scientist, *August 1957*

(the moon landing was just over a decade later, in 1969)

I have not the smallest molecule of faith in aerial navigation other than ballooning.

Lord Kelvin, Victorian physicist and President of the Royal Society, 1896

I have traveled the length and breadth of this country and talked with the best people . . . and I can assure you that data processing is a fad that won't last out the year.

Editor in charge of business books for Prentice Hall publishers, 1957

This "telephone" has too many shortcomings to be seriously considered as a means of communication. The device is inherently of no value to us.

Western Union Telegraph Company, internal memo, 1876

The concept is interesting and well formed, but in order to earn better than a "C," the idea must be feasible.

A Yale University management professor in response to

Fred Smith's paper proposing reliable overnight delivery service.

(Smith went on to found Federal Express)

There is no hope for the fanciful idea of reaching the moon, because of insurmountable barriers to escaping the earth's gravity.

Dr F.R. Moulton, University of Chicago astronomer, 1932

The wireless music box has no imaginable commercial value. Who would pay for a message sent to nobody in particular?

David Sarnoff's associates in response to his urgings
for investment in the radio in the 1920s

While theoretically and technically television may be feasible, commercially and financially it is an impossibility.

Lee DeForest, inventor

Hurrah, boys! We've got them. We'll finish them up and then go home to our station.

General George Custer, before the battle with the Indians
in the Valley of the Little Big Horn, 1876

Radio has no future.

Lord Kelvin, Victorian physicist and President
of the Royal Society, c.1897

The cession of any Colony or Protectorate—save as the result of a crushing defeat in war—is simply unthinkable and would never be accepted by the nation.

Lord Lugard, The Observer *"Sayings of the Week," November 1938*

I must confess that my imagination, in spite even of spurring, refuses to see any sort of submarine doing anything except suffocating its crew and floundering at sea.

H.G. Wells—author of The Time Machine *and* War of the Worlds— *in 1902. U-boats were invented, and were in use by the time of World War I*

Television won't last. It's a flash in the pan.

Mary Somerville, radio presenter, in 1948

I see no good reasons why the views given in this volume should shock the religious sensibilities of anyone.

Charles Darwin, in a preamble to his seminal work on evolution, The Origin Of Species, *which contradicted the creationists' vision-- and turned Victorian society upside down*

[Professor Goddard] does not know the relation between action and reaction and the need to have something better than a vacuum against which to react . . . He seems to lack the basic knowledge ladled out daily in high schools.

The New York Times *(1921), in an editorial discussing Robert Goddard's revolutionary rocket work.*

There are numerous diseases that can be not merely cured, but ultimately abolished when we have once discovered how to use oxygen adequately. Liquefied oxygen will no doubt be our sole disinfectant.

T. Baron Russell, A Hundred Years Hence, *1905*

Man will not be able to fly for at least another fifty years.

Wright brothers, pioneers of powered, manned flight, 1901

The airship probably has many years of life—perhaps at least fifty.

Sir Sefton Brancker, designer of the airship R101, which crashed at Beauvais in France on its maiden flight in 1930—killing, among others, its inventor

Ours has been the first, and doubtless to be the last, to visit this profitless locality.

Lt. Joseph Ives, after visiting the Grand Canyon in 1861

As you may well know, Mr President, "railroad" carriages are pulled at the enormous speed of 15 miles per hour by "engines" which, in addition to endangering life and limb of passengers, roar and snort their way through the countryside, setting fire to crops, scaring the livestock and frightening women and children. The Almighty certainly never intended that people should travel at such breakneck speed.

Martin Van Buren, then governor of New York, in a letter to President Andrew Jackson, 1829

That is the biggest fool thing we have ever done . . . The bomb will never go off.

President Harry S. Truman, shortly after assuming office, when he was briefed on the Manhattan Project to develop atomic weapons. (He subsequently ordered the atomic bombs dropped on Hiroshima and Nagasaki to end World War II with Japan)

No audience will ever be able to take more than ten minutes of animation.

Walt Disney executive, considering the viability
of an animated movie called Snow White and the Seven Dwarves

There is not the slightest indication that nuclear energy will ever be obtainable.
It would mean that the atom would have to be shattered at will.

Albert Einstein, in 1932

The atomic bomb will never go off, and I speak as an expert in explosives.

Admiral William Leahy, on the US Atomic Bomb Project,
to President Truman in 1945

Flight by machines heavier than air is unpractical, and insignificant, if not
utterly impossible.

Simon Newcomb, US astronomer, 1902

Rail travel at high speed is not possible because passengers, unable to breathe,
would die of asphyxia.

Dr Dionysus Lardner, Professor of Natural Philosophy and Astronomy
at University College, London

Lawn tennis, though an excellent game in every respect is, nevertheless, one in
which middle-aged people, especially ladies, cannot engage with satisfaction
to themselves, and its rapidly waning popularity is largely due to this fact.

The Isthmian Book of Croquet, 1899

Airplanes are interesting toys but of no military value.

Ferdinand Foch, Professor of Strategy,
École Supérieure de Guerre, 1911

There will never be a bigger plane built.

A Boeing engineer, after the first flight of the 247,
a twin-engined airplane that held ten people

Louis Pasteur's theory of germs is a ridiculous fiction.

Pierre Pochet, Professor of Physiology at Toulouse,
in The Universe: The Infinitely Great and the Infinitely Small, *1872*

It would be found altogether useless in practice, because the power being
applied in the stern, it would be absolutely impossible to make the vessel
steer.

Sir William Symonds, Surveyor of HM Navy,
on propeller-driven ships, in 1837

Relativity is the moronic brainchild of a mental colic. Voodoo nonsense.

George Francis Gillette, in 1929. Gillette was an advocate
of the 'back-screwing theory of gravity'

The problem with television is that the people must sit and keep their eyes
glued to a screen; the average American family hasn't time for it.

The New York Times, *1939*

We march straight on; we march to victory.

> *Harold, King of England, refusing to parlay before the Batttle of Hastings*
> *in 1066, the outcome of which saw William of Normandy*
> *win the English crown*

No mere machine can replace a reliable and honest clerk.

> *Remington Arms Co., dismissing a newfangled invention*
> *which had been given the name "typewriter"*

Television won't matter in your lifetime or mine.

> *Rex Lambert, Editor of* The Listener *journal, writing in 1936*

Speaking movies are impossible. When a century has passed, all thought of our so-called "talking pictures" will have been abandoned. It will never be possible to synchronize the voice with the picture.

> *D.W. Griffiths, movie mogul, ruling out the possibility*
> *of talking films in 1926*

We have a saying in Iran: "The dogs bark but the caravan continues." People can bark and it will not bother us. Why should it?

> *The Shah of Iran, in 1979*

Anybody can make a mistake.

> *Italian doctor representing a small religious cult who had shut themselves in a*
> *cabin on Mont Blanc, believing the end of the world would come about . . . at*
> *1.45 p.m. The doctor was speaking (sheepishly) at 1.56 p.m, July 1959*

Probably Mr Marconi will succeed in signalling without wires to America from his laboratory at Poole, but the cable companies have no fears, for the rate of transmission in aetheric telegraphy is much slower than where wires are employed.

Article in a London newspaper, c. 1900

It possesses many advantages over morphine . . . It is not hypnotic and there is no danger of acquiring the habit.

James R.L. Daly's analysis of a new drug, diacetylmorphine –
a.k.a. heroin–in the Boston Medical and Surgical Journal of 1900

It can be exploited for a certain time as a scientific curiosity, but apart from that it has no commercial value whatsoever.

August Lumière on his invention—the moving picture projector

A pretty mechanical toy.

Lord Kitchener, British Secretary of State for war, c.1917
dismissing the tank as a weapon of war

No-one knows more about this mountain than Harry. And it don't dare blow up on him!

Harry Truman (not the US president), owner of a mountain cabin near
Mount St. Helens. The "inactive"–or so he thought—volcano blew up
a few days later, engulfing it and its owner

This plane is the greatest single step forward in combat aircraft in several decades.

> *Robert McNamara, then US Secretary of Defense, announcing the revolutionary F-111 in 1964 (the aircraft then rewarded his confidence by dropping out of the sky with disconcerting regularity)*

The most ambitious United States endeavor in the years ahead will be the campaign to land men on neighboring Mars. Most experts estimate the task can be accomplished by 1985.

> *Extract from the* Wall Street Journal, *1966*

Very interesting, Whittle, my boy, but it will never work.

> *Cambridge University Aeronautical Engineering Department's response to Frank Whittle, after viewing his pioneering designs for the jet engine*

A collision at sea can ruin your entire day.

> *Thucydides (attrib.) 5th century BC*

By the year 2000, there will be no C, X, or Q in our everyday alphabet . . . They will be abandoned because they are unnecessary. Spelling by sound will have been adopted, first by the newspapers. English will be a language of condensed words expressing condensed ideas, and will be more extensively spoken than any other. Russian will rank second.

> *Extract from the* Ladies Home Journal, *December 1900*

Knife and pain are two words in surgery that must forever be associated.

Alfred Velpeau, French surgeon,
damning the whole concept of anaesthesia in 1839

Four or five frigates will do the business without any military force.

Lord North, addressing the House of Commons at the outbreak of the
American Revolution (1774)

You will be home before the leaves have fallen from the trees.

Kaiser Wilhelm, encouraging departing
German troops at the outbreak of World War I

War is the most exciting and dramatic thing in life. In fighting to death you feel
terribly relaxed when you manage to come through.

General Moshe Dayan, February 1972

Among the great men who have philosophized about [the action of the tides],
the one who has surprised me most is Kepler. He was a person of
independent genius, [but he] became interested in the action of the moon on
the water, and in other occult phenomena, and similar.

Galileo Galilei

We just won't have arthritis in 2000.

Dr William Clark, president of the Arthritis Foundation, 1966

Politics—the soundbite bites back

Democracy is the art and science of running the circus from the monkey cage.

H.L.Mencken

Politics gives guys so much power that they tend to behave badly around women. I hope I never get into that.

Bill Clinton, avant-Lewinsky

That's not a lie, it's a terminological inexactitude.

Alexander Haig, US Secretary of State

I have opinions of my own—strong opinions—but I don't always agree with them.

George W. Bush

I regret to say that we of the FBI are powerless to act in cases of oral-genital intimacy, unless it has in some way obstructed interstate commerce.

J. Edgar Hoover, former FBI Director

Sure there are dishonest men in local government. But there are dishonest men in national government too.

Richard Nixon

I got tired listening to one million dollars here, one million dollars there. It's so petty.

Imelda Marcos, former First Lady of the Philippines and world-renowned shoe collector

Once you've seen one ghetto, you've seen them all.

Spiro T. Agnew, former Governor of Maryland and Vice-President under Nixon

What's not fine is, rarely is the question asked: Is our children learning?

George W Bush, 14 January 2000

We lead in exporting jobs.

Dan Quayle, addressing the Chamber of Commerce of Evansville, Indiana (where three large companies had been sent to the wall in the previous four years). He corrected himself, substituting the word "products" for "jobs"

I have said that I'm not running and I'm having a great time being Pres—being a first-term senator.

Hillary Clinton, on whether she had any presidential ambitions

I'm praying, of course, that Hillary will win. If she doesn't—Lord, I'll have to call
Revlon again.

> *Vernon Jordan, friend and advisor to Bill Clinton, on Hillary's New York State*
> *bid. (Jordan was criticized during the Clinton impeachment trial for having*
> *called Revlon to secure Monica Lewinsky a job)*

I never trust a man unless I've got his pecker in my pocket.

> *Lyndon B. Johnson*

The only way the French are going in is if we tell them we found truffles in Iraq.

> *Dennis Miller, on France's refusal to back the US-led invasion of Iraq, 2003*

James Bond is a man of honor, a symbol of real value to the free world.

> *Ronald Reagan*

When I was young and irresponsible, I was young and irresponsible.

> *George W. Bush*

Last time I saw (Clinton) he was swinging on the chandelier in the Oval Office
with a brassiere around his head, Viagra in one hand and a Bible in the other,
and he was torn between good and evil.

> *Congressman James A. Traficant, Jr. (Democrat, Ohio)*

I am honored today to begin my first term as the governor of Baltimore—that is,
Maryland.

> *William Donald Schaefer, in his inaugural address*

Every kind of mix you can have. I have a black, I have a woman, two Jews and a cripple.

> *James Watt, US Interior Secretary in 1983, describing the make-up of a five-member commission set up by himself. (Unsurprisingly, he found himself relieved of his post)*

This President is going to lead us out of this recovery. It will happen.

> *Vice-President Dan Quayle at a campaign stop*

Walter Mondale (Democratic candidate): George Bush doesn't have the manhood to apologize.

> *George H.W. Bush (Republican candidate): Well, on the manhood thing, I'll put mine up against his any time*

We have, of course, often done it before, but never on a pavement outside a hotel in Eastbourne. We have done it in various rooms in one way or another at various functions. It is perfectly genuine—and normal and right—so to do.

> *William Whitelaw (on kissing Margaret Thatcher) in 1975*

Freedom's untidy.

> *Donald Rumsfeld, US Defense Secretary, on looting in Baghdad following the US-led invasion of Iraq, 2003*

You're free. And freedom is beautiful. And, you know, it'll take time to restore chaos and order—order out of chaos. But we will.

> *George W. Bush, Washington DC, April 13, 2003*

Just one for the gibbet.

> *Ronald Reagan towards the end of his presidency, during which he had been*
> *known for the phrase, "Just one for the Gipper"*

Buzz Lukens took that fateful step . . .

> *Dan Quayle, confusing the sexual assaulter/congressman*
> *with astronaut Buzz Aldrin.*

The President has kept all of the promises he intended to keep.

> *George Stephanopolous, Clinton aide, speaking on* Larry King Live

I am on the right wing of the middle of the road with a strong radical bias.

> *Anthony Wedgwood-Benn, speaking in the mid-1950s*

Rural Americans are real Americans. There's no doubt about that. You can't always be sure with other Americans. Not all of them are real.

> *Dan Quayle*

Laura and I really don't realize how bright our children is sometimes until we get an objective analysis.

> *George W. Bush,* Meet the Press, *15 April 2000*

This is still a dangerous world. It's a world of madmen and uncertainty and potential mental losses.

> *George W. Bush, at a South Carolina oyster roast,*
> *quoted in the* Financial Times, *14 January 2000*

All this notion of gollies being derogatory to black people is nonsense.

Bristol Councillor Richard Eddy, on BBC Radio Bristol,
September 2001 (following which statement, he was forced to resign as Deputy
Leader of the Tory group)

I haven't committed a crime. What I did was fail to comply with the law.

David Dinkins, former mayor of New York City, defending himself against
accusations that he had failed to pay his taxes

When my sister and I were growing up, there was never any doubt in our minds
that men and women were equal, if not more so.

Al Gore, to an audience composed mostly of women

I was recently on a tour of Latin America, and the only regret I have was that I
didn't study Latin harder in school so I could converse with those people.

Dan Quayle (attrib.—frequently)

What I don't like about politics is the disruption to one's family life.

Cecil Parkinson, in May 1983—then a Conservative cabinet minister,
as yet untouched by the scandal of his relationship
(and fathering of a child) with his secretary, Miss Sarah Keays

Redefining the role of the United States from enablers to keep the peace to
enablers to keep the peace from peacekeepers is going to be an assignment.

George W. Bush

Polacks.

Spiro T. Agnew, on Polish-Americans, 1968

I will have a foreign-handed foreign policy.

George W. Bush

My friends, no matter how rough the road may be, we can and we will never, never surrender to what is right.

Dan Quayle, speaking to the Christian Coalition about the need for sexual abstinence if AIDS is to be curbed

For seven and a half years I've worked alongside President Reagan. We've had triumphs. Made some mistakes. We've had some sex . . . uh, setbacks.

George H.W. Bush

You can tell a lot about a fellow's character by the way he eats jelly beans.

President Reagan, January 1981

I'm not against the blacks and a lot of the good blacks will attest to that.

Evan Mecham, then Governor of Arizona

[The Democrats had] cramped down on any discussion of individual initiatives.

George H.W. Bush

If Lincoln was alive today, he'd roll over in his grave.

Gerald R. Ford, US President

The caribou love it. They rub against it and they have babies. There are more caribou in Alaska than you can shake a stick at.

George H.W. Bush, on the Alaska pipeline

I strongly support the feeding of children.

President Gerald R. Ford, stating the obvious when commenting on the school dinner program

I know how hard it is for you to put food on your family.

George W. Bush, talking about putting food on the plates of youngsters, in Greater Nashua, New Hampshire, 27 January 2000

The American people would not want to know of any misquotes that Dan Quayle may or may not make.

Dan Quayle

I think they have misunderestimated me.

George W. Bush's response to the question, "What do you think of citizens saying you are too religious?" in People *magazine*

Although in public I refer to him as Mr. Vice-President, in private I call him George . . . When I talked to him on the phone yesterday, I called him George rather than Mr Vice-President. But, in public, it's Mr Vice-President, because that's who he is.

Dan Quayle

Now we are trying to get unemployment to go up, and I think we are going to succeed.

Ronald Reagan, in 1982

The fact that he relies on facts —says things that are not factual—are going to undermine his campaign.

George W. Bush, on Al Gore,
quoted in The New York Times, *4 March 2000*

I didn't like it and I didn't inhale it.

President Bill Clinton, boxing around the question of him having smoked
marijuana when he was a student

I've changed my style somewhat, as you know. I'm less . . . I pontificate less, although it may be hard to tell it from this show. And I'm more interacting with people.

George W. Bush, Meet The Press, *NBC, 13 February 2000*

It's no exaggeration to say that the undecideds could go one way or another.

George H. W. Bush, at a campaign rally,
October 1988

I think there is a Trojan horse lurking in the weeds trying to pull a fast one on the American people.

George W. Bush in a live, radio, phone-in, mixing his metaphors
while "discussing" US foreign policy

You cannot be President of the United States if you don't have faith. Remember Lincoln, going to his knees in times of trial and the Civil War and all that stuff. You can't be. And we are blessed. So don't feel sorry for—don't cry for me Argentina.

George H.W. Bush, mangling his syntax and
muddling his allusions

This is a world that is much more uncertain than the past. In the past we were certain, we were certain it was us versus the Russians in the past. We were certain, and therefore we had huge nuclear arsenals aimed at each other to keep the peace . . . You see, even though it's an uncertain world, we're certain of some things.

George W. Bush

Add one little bit on the end . . . Think of "potatoe," how's it spelled? You're right phonetically, but what else? There ya go . . . all right!

Vice-President Dan Quayle "correcting" a student's (correct) spelling of the word
"potato" during a spelling bee at an elementary school in the Luis Munoz Rivera
School in Trenton, New Jersey

I should have caught the mistake on that spelling bee card. But as Mark Twain once said, "You should never trust a man who has only one way to spell a word."

Vice-President Dan Quayle, actually quoting from
President Andrew Jackson

I should have remembered that was Andrew Jackson who said that, since he
got his nickname "Stonewall" by vetoing bills passed by Congress.

Vice-President Dan Quayle, confusing Andrew Jackson with
Confederate General Thomas J. "Stonewall" Jackson, who actually
got his nickname at the first Battle of Bull Run

(It's) time for the human race to enter the solar system.

Dan Quayle, speaking about the notion of a manned mission to Mars

You know, if I were a single man, I might ask that mummy out. That's a good-
looking mummy.

President Bill Clinton, appraising "Juanita", a newly-discovered Inca mummy on
display at the National Geographic Museum.

George W. Bush: I was not elected to serve one party.

Jon Stewart: You were not elected.

George W. Bush: I have something else to ask you, to ask every American. I ask
you to pray for this great nation.

Jon Stewart: We're way ahead of you.

Exchange on The Daily Show.

I didn't go down there with any plan for the Americas, or anything. I went down
to find out from them and (learn) their views. You'd be surprised. They're all
individual countries.

Ronald Reagan, responding in 1982 to a question about whether
his five-day Latin American trip had changed his outlook on the region

I would give up half—nay, the whole of the constitution to preserve the remainder.

Sir Boyle Roche, eighteenth-century member of parliament

The United States has much to offer the third world war.

Ronald Reagan, in 1975 (meaning the Third World);
he made the same mistake several times

Facts are stupid things.

Ronald Reagan, addressing the Republican National Convention in 1988. He
was misquoting John Adams who, in 1778, wrote, "Facts are stubborn things."
Reagan repeated the mistake several time

For NASA, space is still a high priority.

Dan Quayle, 1990

The senator (McCain) has got to understand if he's going to have—he can't have it both ways. He can't take the high horse and then claim the low road.

George W. Bush to reporters in Florence, South Carolina, about his Republican
nomination opponent, 17 February 2000

It is clear our nation is reliant upon big foreign oil. More and more of our imports come from overseas.

George W. Bush, September 2000

Gentlemen, the apple of discord has been thrown into our midst; and if it be not nipped in the bud, it will burst into a conflagration which will deluge the world.

Sir Boyle Roche, eighteenth-century member of parliament

They asked me to go in front of the Reagans. I'm not used to going in front of President Reagan, so we went out behind the Bushes.

Dan Quayle

People that are really very weird can get into sensitive positions and have tremendous impact on history.

Dan Quayle

A zebra does not change its spots.

Al Gore, attacking President Bush in 1992

I'm glad I'm not Brezhnev. Being the Russian leader in the Kremlin, you never know if someone's tape-recording what you say.

President Richard Nixon

Bank failures are caused by depositors who don't deposit enough money to cover losses due to mismanagement.

Dan Quayle

UN goodwill may be a bottomless pit, it's by no means limitless.

John Major, British Prime Minister

I think anybody who doesn't think I'm smart enough to handle this job is
underestimating.

George W. Bush on his ability to head the world's superpower

The problem with the French is that they don't have a word for "entrepreneur."

George W. Bush's aside to British Prime Minister Tony Blair during a conference
attended by French President Jacques Chirac; the discussion was economics
and, in particular, the decline of the French economy

Helen Thomas (reporter): If you had it to do over again, would you put on the
nation's uniform?

President Bill Clinton: If I had to do it over again, I might answer the questions a
little better. You know I've been in public life a long time, and no one had ever
questioned my role.

Let me say it one more time. It is ill-rel-e-vant.

Senator Dan Quayle, responding testily to reiterated questions about his
parents' involvement in the John Birch Society

It is not Reaganesque to support a tax plan that is Clinton in nature.

George W. Bush, Los Angeles, 23 February 2000

I was provided with additional input that was radically different from the truth.
I assisted in furthering that version.

Colonel Oliver North, from his testimony during the
Iran–Contra scandal

I've read about foreign policy and studied—I know the number of continents.

Governor George Wallace, US presidential campaign, 1968

The purpose of government is to rein in the rights of the people.

Bill Clinton, during an interview on MTV in 1993

If you let that sort of thing go on, your bread and butter will be cut right out
from under your feet.

Ernest Bevin, former British Foreign Minister

It could have been spinach dip or something.

Monica Lewinsky, on the famous stain on her dress

China is a big country, inhabited by many Chinese.

Charles de Gaulle, former French President

I think we agree, the past is over.

George W. Bush, during his meeting with John McCain,
Dallas Morning News, *10 May 2000*

Things are more like they are now than they ever were before.

Dwight D. Eisenhower, former US President

If you've seen one redwood tree, you've seen them all.

Ronald Reagan (aspiring forestry expert)

Please could they switch off now, use the minimum of appliances, keep the
lights off in any room that's not occupied, switch off electric heaters, keep one
bar on if one bar will do—don't switch on two bars—and so on. (There are) so
many things that people could do to reduce the consumption of electricity . . .
You don't even (need to) do your teeth with the light on. You can do it in the
dark.

*Soundbite from a broadcast by the British Minister for Energy, Patrick Jenkin,
during the energy crisis and Three-Day-Week resulting from the miners' strike in
1974. He was photographed using his plug-in electric shaver by candlelight.*
From Sayings of the Century, *by Nigel Rees*

When more and more people are thrown out of work, unemployment results.
*Calvin Coolidge, former US President, discussing the economic
climate in the United States in 1931*

It is necessary for me to establish a winner image. Therefore I have to beat
somebody.

Richard Nixon

Justice is incidental to law and order.
J. Edgar Hoover, former FBI Director

We are not without accomplishment. We have managed to distribute poverty
equally.

Nguyen Co Thatch, ex-Foreign Minister of Vietnam

I'm not going to focus on what I have done in the past, what I stand for, what I articulate to the American people. The American people will judge me on what I am saying and what I have done in the last twelve years in the Congress.

Dan Quayle

If two wrongs don't make a right, try three.

Richard Nixon

I promise you a police car on every sidewalk.

Marion Barry, Mayor of Washington DC

Unfortunately, the people of Louisiana are not racists.

Dan Quayle

The plea for security could well become a cloak for errors, misjudgements and other failings of government.

Richard Nixon—prophetic words, uttered in May 1961

What's a man got to do to get in the top fifty?

President Bill Clinton, reacting to a survey of journalists that ranked the Lewinksy scandal as the 53rd most significant story of the century

Oh, that was just an accident that happened.

President Richard Nixon, on the missing eighteen minutes on the Watergate tapes

My fellow Americans. I'm pleased to tell you today that I've signed legislation that will outlaw Russia forever. (Laughter.) We begin bombing in five minutes. (Laughter.)

> *Ronald Reagan, during a 1984 press conference about negotiations with Russia over nuclear arms reduction, in what he thought was a sound check for the radio engineers. The Russian ambassador was sitting nearby*

I was raised in the West. The West of Texas. It's pretty close to California. In more ways than Washington DC is close to California.

> *George W. Bush, quoted in the* Los Angeles Times, *8 April 2000*

We are not going to send American boys nine or ten thousand miles to do what Asian boys ought to be doing for themselves.

> *Lydon B. Johnson, US President, 1964*

We're all capable of mistakes, but I do not care to enlighten you on the mistakes we may or may not have made.

> *Dan Quayle*

It's like an Alcatraz around my neck.

> *Thomas M. Menino, Boston Mayor, on the shortage of parking spaces in his city. He meant albatross, of course*

Every prime minister needs a Willie.

> *Margaret Thatcher, referring to Lord William Whitelaw*

We must not prejudge the past.

Lord Whitelaw

If you're sick and tired of the politics of cynicism and polls and principles, come
and join this campaign.

George W. Bush, Hilton Head, South Carolina, 16 February 2000

No woman in my time will be Prime Minister or Chancellor or Foreign
Secretary—not the top jobs. Anyway, I wouldn't want to be Prime Minister.
You have to give yourself one hundred per cent.

Margaret Thatcher, interviewed in the Sunday Telegraph *in October 1969, when
she was Shadow Spokesman on Education—ten years later, on 4 May 1979, she
became the first woman PM in British history*

The American people's expectations are that we will fail. Our mission is to
exceed their expectations.

*George W. Bush at one of his first televised cabinet meetings
in an opening speech to the cabinet*

It will be years—not in my time—before a woman will become Prime Minister.

Margaret Thatcher, in 1974

Keep good relations with the Grecians.

*George W. Bush (unfortunately, apart from not calling the Greek nation's people
"Greeks," the word "Grecian" also appears in a men's hair product for greying
hair). Quoted in* The Economist, *12 June 1999*

I feel that this is my first year, that next year is an election year, that the third year is the mid-point, and that the fourth year is the last chance I'll have to make a record since the last two years; I'll be a candidate again. Everything I do in those last two years will be posturing for the election. But right now I don't have to do that.

Dan Quayle

You have to fight a battle more than once to win it.

Margaret Thatcher

Only one thing would be worse than the status quo. And that would be for the status quo to become the norm.

Elizabeth Dole in 1999, during a campaign speech

The Internet is a great way to get on the Net.

Bob Dole, Republican presidential candiate

We are a grandmother.

Margaret Thatcher, on learning that her son Mark and his wife were going to have a baby. (The more acceptable use of the "Royal We" is that much employed by HRH Queen Elizabeth II)

I don't mind how much my ministers talk, as long as they do what I say.

Margaret Thatcher

If I listened to Michael Dukakis long enough, I would be convinced that we're in an economic downturn and people are homeless and going without food and medical attention and that we've got to do something about the unemployed.

Ronald Reagan

I love sports. Whenever I can, I always watch the Detroit Tigers (baseball team) on the radio.

Gerald R. Ford, US President

We expect them (Salvadorian officials) to work toward the elimination of human rights in accordance with the pursuit of justice.

Dan Quayle

I understand small business growth. I was one.

George W. Bush, quoted in New York Daily News, *19 February 2000*

You read what Disraeli had to say. I don't remember what he said. He said something. He's no longer with us.

Bob Dole adding to the sum of knowledge on the Monica Lewinsky affair during the Clinton administration

I did not have sexual relations with that woman.

President Bill Clinton, denying sexual shenanigans with White House intern Monica Lewinsky

We are the boiling pot. We have open arms.

Senator Bob Dole, discussing the US "melting pot"

The President doesn't want any yes-men and yes-women around him. When he says no, we all say no.

Elizabeth Dole, then aide to Ronald Reagan

First I'd like to spank all the teachers . . .

George W. Bush, in an address to American teachers on NBC. (A short pause followed, during which a flicker of recognition passed over his face as his mistake dawned. Then he continued with his speech)

President Carter speaks loudly and carries a fly spotter, a fly swasher—it's been a long day.

Gerald R. Ford

Bush: First of all, Cinco de Mayo is not the independence day. That's Dieciséis de Septiembre, and . . .
Interviewer: What's that in English?
Bush: Fifteenth of September.

Exchange between Bush and interviewer on Hardball *on MSNBC, 31 May 2000 (Dieciséis de Septiembre is September 16 . . .)*

No, I eat three square meals a day.

George W. Bush's response to a reporter who asked if he was dyslexic

I'm not going to have some reporters pawing through our papers. We are the President.

Hillary Clinton, on the release of subpoenaed documents

We'll let the other countries of the world be the peacekeepers and the great
country called America be the pacemakers.

George W. Bush

To you, and to the people you represent, the great people of the government of
Israel . . . Egypt, excuse me.

*President Gerald R. Ford, proposing a toast at a state dinner held in his honor by
the Egyptian leader, Anwar el-Sadat, December 1975*

Doesn't the fight for survival also justify swindle and theft? In self-defense,
anything goes.

Imelda Marcos, former First Lady of the Philippines

Neither in French nor in English nor in Mexican.

*George W. Bush at the Summit of the Americas in Quebec City, when asked to
answer questions about what had taken place. He replied that he would not in
any of the mentioned languages (of which Mexican is not one)*

Quite frankly, teachers are the only profession that teach our children.

Dan Quayle, US Vice-President, 18 September 1990

I have had great financial sex.

*Ross Perot in a speech; he was aiming to say
"I have had great financial success"*

We cannot let terrorists and rogue nations hold this nation hostile or hold our allies hostile.

George W. Bush on the matter of US national security, 21 August 2000

Grass doesn't grow on a busy street.

William Hague, former British Conservative Party leader,
reflecting on (his own) baldness

I don't think that "greedy" even now is a word I would attach—but I think we went over the top a bit.

Disgraced MP, Neil Hamilton, during the Al Fayed libel case

I was a hard-working wife. I worked hard all the time, in the constituency and elsewhere. I had to do the shopping, washing, all the food preparation; and to be at the hotel, it was luxurious, and wonderful, and yes, I enjoyed it.

Christine Hamilton, describing her Al Fayed-funded stay at the Paris Ritz.

Outside of the killings, (Washington) has one of the lowest crime rates in the country.

Marion Barry, Mayor of Washington DC

If crime went down one hundred per cent it would still be fifty times higher than it should be.

John Bowman, commenting on the
high crime rate in Washington DC

Hawaii is a unique state. It is a small state. It is a state that is by itself. It is—it is different from the other 49 states. Well, all states are different, but it's got a particularly unique situation.

Dan Quayle

I'm no linguist, but I've been told that in the Russian language there isn't even a word for freedom.

Ronald Reagan, in 1985 (there is—and it's svoboda)

The best cure for insomnia is to get a lot of sleep.

S. I. Hayakawa, US Senator

Wherever I have gone in this country, I have found Americans.

Alf Landon (speaking in the United States), during a speech during his presidential campaign against Franklin D. Roosevelt

It isn't pollution that's harming the environment. It's the impurities in our air and water that are doing it.

Dan Quayle

The right to suffer is one of the joys of a free economy.

Howard Pyle, aide to President Eisenhower, commenting on the unemployment situation in Detroit

There is a mandate to impose a voluntary return to traditional values.

Ronald Reagan

Devaluation.

> *George W Bush, making a passing comment about the Yen during a visit to*
> *Japan, saying the currency was subject to "devaluation." This word, when*
> *reported, prompted a virtual crash on the Japanese stock market a few hours*
> *later, until one of the President's aides explained that Mr Bush had actually*
> *meant "deflation" of the Yen*

The streets are safe in Philadelphia—it's only the people who make
them unsafe.

> *Frank Rizzo, ex-Police Chief and Mayor of Philadelphia*

Putting subliminable [sib-lim-in-a-bal] messages into commercials is absurd.

> *George W. Bush, countering claims that he put subliminal*
> *messages in a commercial*

A man could not be in two places at the same time unless he were a bird.

> *Sir Boyle Roche, eighteenth-century member of parliament from*
> *Tralee, Ireland–known for his malapropisms*

I'm not indecisive. Am I indecisive?

> *Jim Scheibel, Mayor of St. Paul, Minnesota.*

Wait a minute! I'm not interested in agriculture. I want the military stuff.

> *Senator William Scott, during a briefing in which officials*
> *began telling him about missile silos*

One word sums up probably the responsibility of any Vice-President, and that
one word is "to be prepared."

Dan Quayle, December 1989

This is the epitaph I want on my tomb: Here lies one of the most intelligent
animals who ever appeared on the face of the earth.

Benito Mussolini

God is love. I have loved. Therefore, I will go to heaven.

Imelda Marcos, former First Lady of the Philippines

Gerald Ford is a communist.

Ronald Reagan (he meant to say congressman)

That's the way the cookie bounces.

Vic Schiro, New Orleans Mayor—famous for his malapropisms,
called "Schiroisms"

And America needs a military where our breast and brightest are proud to
serve, and proud to stay.

George W. Bush's remark to the troops of Fort Stewart, Georgia

I do not like this word bomb. It is not a bomb. It is a device which is exploding.

Jacques Le Blanc, French Ambassador to New Zealand
describing France's nuclear testing in 1995

There are two kinds of truth. There are real truths, and there are made-up truths.

> *Marion Barry, Mayor of Washington DC, on his arrest for drug use*

It's clearly a budget. It's got a lot of numbers in it.

> *George W. Bush, Reuters, 5 May 2000*

Fifty years on from now, Britain will still be the country of long shadows on county (cricket) grounds, warm beer, invincible green suburbs, dog lovers and old maids cycling to Holy Communion through the morning mist.

> *John Major, British Prime Minister, giving us a small insight as to why he hasn't turned his hand to novel writing*

When I have been asked during these last weeks who caused the riots and the killing in Los Angeles, my answer has been direct and simple: Who is to blame for the riots? The rioters are to blame. Who is to blame for the killings? The killers are to blame.

> *Dan Quayle*

The theories—the ideas she expressed about equality of results within legislative bodies and with—by outcome, by decisions made by legislative bodies, ideas related to proportional voting as a general remedy, not in particular cases where the circumstances make that a feasible idea . . .

> *Al Gore*

Education is my top priority. However, education is not my top priority.

George W. Bush

You mean there are two Koreas?

Richard Kneip, US Ambassador Designate to Singapore, upon being asked his opinion of the North–South Korean divide during congressional hearings

I am not a chauvinist, obviously . . . I believe in women's rights for every woman but my own.

Harold Washington, Chicago Mayor

I have been sitting here and listening to you for an hour, and I am now aware that you are a strong and intelligent man and that you want peace . . . I believe, Mr President, that you can be a very influential force for peace in the Middle East.

Senator Howard Metzenbaum (Democrat, Ohio) in 1990, in a meeting with Iraqi President Saddam Hussein

I am a traditionalist with an appetite for change.

Giscard d'Estaing, French President

I hope that Agnew will be completely exonerated and found guilty of the charges against him.

John Connally, Texas governor, trying to defend his friend Spiro Agnew, Nixon's Vice-President, who was facing charges of tax evasion

Don't believe any false rumors unless you hear them from me.

> *New Orleans Mayor Vic Schiro, uttering arguably his all-time greatest*
> *malapropism while inspecting damage resulting from Hurricane Betsy*

The single most important two things we can do . . .

> *Tony Blair*

If it (deviant behavior) will bring about terrorist bombs, if it'll bring about
earthquakes, tornadoes, and possibly a meteor, it isn't necessarily something
we ought to open our arms to.

> *Pat Robertson*

If Ross Perot runs, that's good for us. If he doesn't run, it's good for us.

> *Dan Quayle, to a reporter. The reporter then enquired what he meant*
> *by this, and was met with the even more bewildering response,*
> *"That's for you to figure out"*

A hobby I enjoy is mapping the human genome. I hope one day I can clone
another Dick Cheney. Then I won't have to do anything.

> *George W. Bush, at the Gridiron dinner*

Always be sincere, even if you don't mean it.

> *Harry S. Truman, US President*

We're going to have the best-educated American people in the world.

> *Dan Quayle, September 1988*

Waste of time. They're all just a load of balladonnas.

Lord Blyton (1899–1987), English politican (he meant, "primadonnas")

Well, I think if you say you're going to do something and don't do it, that's trustworthiness.

George W. Bush

This is a great day for France!

Richard Nixon, said whilst attending President De Gaulle's funeral

I don't see, Mr Speaker, why we should put ourselves out of the way to serve posterity. What has posterity ever done for us? (Laughter in the House) By posterity, sir, I do not mean our ancestors, but those who are to come immediately after them.

Sir Boyle Roche, eighteenth-century member of parliament

I love California, I practically grew up in Phoenix.

Dan Quayle (Phoenix is in Arizona)

Once I was deflowered, they weren't interested in me.

President Bill Clinton, having been pursued by a group of monkeys before he discarded his garland on a tour in India

Deep down I'm a very shallow person.

Charles Haughey, Irish Taoiseach (Prime Minister)

Illegitimacy is something we should talk about in terms of not having it.

Dan Quayle, May 1992

Interviewer: Can you name the President of Chechnya?

Bush: No. Can you?

(Two questions, about the Presidents of Taiwan and Pakistan followed)

Bush: The new Pakistani General, he's just been elected. He's not elected—this

guy took over office. He appears he'll bring stability to

the country . . .

Interviewer: And can you name him?

Bush: General, I can. Name the General.

Interviewer: And it's . . .?

Bush: General . . .

Interviewer: And the Prime Minister of India?

Bush: Er . . . The new Prime Minister of India is . . . er . . . No. Can you name the

Foreign Minister of Mexico?

Exchange between Andy Hiller, local TV journalist,
and George W. Bush, on WHDH in Boston, 1999

Who are these guys?

Vice-President Al Gore, referring (on camera, to CNN viewers) to the busts of
Washington, Franklin, Lafayette and Jefferson on a tour of Monticello (former
home of Thomas Jefferson)

I think incest can be handled as a family matter within the family.

Representative Jay Dickey (Republican, Arkansas) defending his position
against abortion, even in the case of rape or incest

Ladies and Gentlemen, it is my honor to introduce you to the governor of this
great state, the Honorable John J. McKeithen and his lovely wife, Marjorie.
Look how beautiful she is—every wrinkle on her face is glowing.

Vic Schiro, New Orleans mayor, famous for his malapropisms,
called "Schiroisms"

The most important job is not to be Governor, or First Lady, in my case.

George W. Bush, Pella, Iowa. Quoted in the San Antonio Express News,
30 January 2000

The other day (the President) said, I know you've had some rough times, and I
want to do something that will show the nation what faith that I have in you,
in your maturity and sense of responsibility. (Pause.) Would you like a puppy?

Dan Quayle

I smell a rat, I see it floating in the air. But mark me, I shall yet nip it in the bud.

Sir Boyle Roche, eighteenth-century member of parliament

How do you know if you don't measure if you have a system that simply suckles
kids through?

George W. Bush, on the need to measure educational achievement, Beaufort

We have a firm commitment to NATO; we are a part of NATO. We have a firm commitment to Europe. We are a part of Europe.

Dan Quayle

I just wanna say . . . you husbands and wives, if you wanna get along together, you gotta get one of these tantrum bicycles.

Richard Daley, Mayor of Chicago

I have made good judgements in the past. I have made good judgements in the future.

Dan Quayle

This is the greatest week in the history of the world since the Creation.

President Richard Nixon, greeting Neil Armstrong and Buzz Aldrin—the first men to land on the moon—somewhat over-enthusiastically on their return from their historic voyage

The important question is: "How many hands have I shaked?"

George W. Bush, answering a question about why he hadn't spent more time in New Hampshire. Quoted in The New York Times, *23 October 1999*

(A) Great President who might have been—Hubert Horatio Hornblower.

President Jimmy Carter becoming gaffe-prone in August 1980 during the lead-up to re-election time. He was thinking of the great democrat Hubert H. Humphrey, who never made it as far as the White House

I'm honored. I appreciate his strong statement . . . He understands I want to ensure our relationship with our most important neighbor to the north of us, Canadians, is strong. We will work closely together.

George W. Bush's response in March 2000 to a Canadian comedian posing as a reporter, and asking for his response to the endorsement from Canada's Prime Minister Jean Poutine. (The Canadian Prime Minister at the time was Jean Chretien, Poutine being a popular Canadian snack consisting of French fries covered in cheese curd and gravy)

When a great many people are unable to find work, unemployment results.

Herbert Hoover, candidate for the US presidency in 1928

Speaking as a man, it's not a woman's issue. Us men are tired of losing our women.

Dan Quayle, talking about raising breast cancer awareness

There will be no whitewash in the White House.

President Richard Nixon, April 1973, as the Watergate scandal loomed

I would like to thank Nasal Beard for that warm welcome.

George H.W. Bush, thanking Hazel Beard, Mayor of Shreveport, Louisiana, in 1992

Verbosity leads to unclear, inarticulate things.

Dan Quayle, November 1988

You know the one thing that's wrong with this country? Everyone gets a chance
    to have their fair say.

Bill Clinton, speaking from the White House, 29 May 1993

Families is where we find hope, where wings take dream.

George W. Bush

(People) get the impression that everybody is here for the purpose of feathering
    his nest . . . Not in this administration: not one single man or woman. And I
    say to them. There are many fine careers. This country needs good farmers,
    good businessmen, good plumbers, good carpenters . . .

Farewell speech of Richard Nixon, 9 August 1974,
on his resignation as President of the United States

I desire the Poles carnally.

An interpreter misinterpreting the words of President Carter
on his visit to Warsaw in December 1978

Ich bin ein Berliner.

President John. F. Kennedy's one phrase of German
in his speech to the German people in 1963. It caused amusement, for a
"berliner" is a type of German doughnut. Later, it was suggested to President
Carter that he say to the people of Frankfurt, "Ich bin ein Frankfurter."
Fortunately for him, he resisted the idea

There was no impropriety whatsoever in my acquaintanceship with Miss Keeler.

> *John Profumo, Secretary of State in Harold Macmillan's government.*
> *It was a lie, and resignation and disgrace swiftly followed*

There is no Soviet domination of Eastern Europe and there never will be under a Ford administration . . . I don't believe . . . Romanians consider themselves dominated by the Soviet Union. I don't believe that the Poles consider themselves dominated by the Soviet Union. Each of these countries is independent, autonomous. It has its own territorial integrity. And the United States does not concede that these countries are under the domination of the Soviet Union.

> *President Gerald R. Ford, in a televised debate with presidential*
> *challenger Jimmy Carter in 1976. Forced to account for this unorthodox view,*
> *Ford finally conceded, "I was not as precise as I should have been." From*
> Sayings of the Century, *by Nigel Rees*

Now, I would ask you to join me in a toast to President Figueiredo and to the people of Bolivia—no, that's where I'm going—to the people of Brazil.

> *President Ronald Reagan on a visit to Brazil in December 1982. (His next stop*
> *wasn't Bolivia, but Bogotá, in Colombia)*

We (Republicans) understand the importance of having the bondage between the parent and the child.

> *Dan Quayle*

This is Preservation Month. I appreciate preservation. It's what you do when you run for president. You gotta preserve.

George W. Bush speaking at Fairgrounds Elementary School in
New Hampshire

Gentlemen, get the thing straight once and for all. The policeman isn't there to create disorder; the policeman is there to preserve disorder.

Richard J. Daley, Chicago Mayor, during the infamous 1968 Democratic
Convention, which was disrupted by anti-Vietnam protests

The Jews and Arabs should sit down and settle their differences like good Christians.

Warren Robinson Austin, US politician and diplomat,
commenting on the Middle East crisis

From now on the pound abroad is worth 14 per cent or so less in terms of other currencies. That doesn't mean, of course, that the pound here in Britain, in your pocket or purse or in your bank, has been devalued. What it does mean is that we shall now be able to sell more goods abroad on a competitive basis.

Prime Minister Harold Wilson in a TV address, broadcast on
19 November 1967, following the devaluation of sterling

This is the operative statement. The others are inoperative.

Ronald Ziegler, Press Secretary to Richard Nixon during the
Watergate affair. The phrase became a euphemism for "lie"

It contains a misleading impression, not a lie. I was being economical with the truth.

> *Sir Robert Armstrong, British civil servant giving evidence on behalf of the*
> *British government in an Australian court case, November 1986*

I did not know in 1969 that I would be in this room today, I'll confess.

> *Senator Dan Quayle, responding to questions in 1988 about allegations that he*
> *used family connections to get into the Indiana National Guard*

I'm surprised that a government organization could do it that quickly.

> *Jimmy Carter in Egypt, when told the Great Pyramid had taken*
> *only twenty years to build*

As I look ahead, I am filled with foreboding. Like the Roman, I seem to see the river Tiber foaming with much blood.

> *Enoch Powell in his "rivers of blood" speech to an audience in Birmingham,*
> *April 1968, which called for a halt to immigration. The speech led to his*
> *dismissal from the Shadow Cabinet by the Conservative leader, Edward Heath.*
> *It also provoked a tide of anti-immigrant feeling*

The idea that congressmen would be tainted by accepting money from private industry or private sources is essentially a socialist argument.

> *Newt Gingrich, ex-Speaker of the House*

We ought to make the pie higher.

> *George W. Bush, South Carolina Republican Debate, 15 February 2000*

[The CIA] encourages spouses of intelligence or military agency employees to cooperate with federal investigators in cases where they know or suspect their government-employed husbands or wives are engaged in espionage. Under this provision, the spouse who cooperates in the prosecution or conviction of his or her spouse beloved would be eligible for spousal benefits for life.

CIA proposal, widely reported in the US press

We must all hear the universal call to like your neighbor just like you like to be liked yourself.

George W. Bush, at a South Carolina oyster roast. Quoted in the
Financial Times, *14 January 2000*

Welcome to President Bush, Mrs. Bush, and my fellow astronauts.

Dan Quayle, addressing his audience at the 20th anniversary
of the moon landing, 1989

A certain anonymous writer named Junius.

Sir Boyle Roche, eighteenth-century member of parliament

(They are) the same people that would be homos in the military.

Randy Cunningham, (Republican, California) having a go at
the supporters of clean water

I don't read books. I write them.

Henry Kissinger

We should respect Mexico's rights to chart its own independent course,
provided the course is not antagonistic to our interests.

Richard Nixon, in an oxymoronic turn of phrase

I prefer beef.

*Robert Muldoon, New Zealand Premier, turning his nose up at his nation's
number one export—lamb*

It is wonderful to be back here in the great state of Chicago.

Dan Quayle

How can a guy this politically immature expect to be President?

*Franklin D. Roosevelt Jr. on John F. Kennedy's
attempt to become President*

We both use Colgate toothpaste.

*President George W. Bush, asked what he and British Prime Minister
Tony Blair might have in common (the reporter suggested sport,
maybe, music, or religion), February 2001*

It's exciting to have a real crisis on your hands, when you have spent half your
political life dealing with humdrum issues like the environment.

Margaret Thatcher on the Falklands conflict

I did not have three thousand pairs of shoes. I had one thousand and sixty.

Imelda Marcos, former First Lady of the Philippines

I hope I stand for anti-bigotry, anti-Semitism, anti-racism. This is what drives me.

George H.W. Bush

You know, your nose looks just like Danny Thomas's.

Ronald Reagan, addressing the Lebanese Foreign Minister

This isn't a man who is leaving with his head between his legs.

Dan Quayle

Nixon has been sitting in the White House while George McGovern has been exposing himself to the people of the United States.

Frank Licht, then governor of Rhode Island, campaigning for McGovern in 1972

I want it to be said that the Bush administration was a results-oriented administration because I believe the results of focusing our attention and energy on teaching children to read and having an education system that's responsive to the child and to the parents, as opposed to mired in a system that refuses to change, will make America what we want it to be – a more literate and hopefuller country.

George W. Bush, January 2001

Approximately 80 per cent of our air pollution stems from hydrocarbons
released by vegetation, so let's not go overboard in setting and enforcing
tough emission standards from man-made sources.

*Ronald Reagan, in his groundbreaking "trees cause more pollution than
automobiles" speech, September 1980*

I favor the Civil Rights Act of 1964, and it must be enforced at gunpoint if
necessary.

Ronald Reagan, October 1965

I want real loyalty. I want someone who will kiss my ass in Macy's window, and
say it smells like roses.

Lyndon B. Johnson

I always figured the American public wanted a solemn ass for President. So I
went along with them.

Calvin Coolidge, former US President

I am a great mayor; I am an upstanding Christian man. I am an intelligent man. I
am a deeply-educated man. I am a humble man.

Marion Barry, Mayor of Washington DC

One of the great things about books is that sometimes there are some fantastic
pictures.

George W. Bush

There is no question of eroding any national sovereignty; there is no blueprint
for a federal Europe. There are some in this country who fear that in going
into Europe, we shall in some way sacrifice independence and sovereignty.
These fears I need hardly say are completely unjustified.

Former British Prime Minister, Edward Heath, 1972

I have never understood why public opinion about European ideas should be
taken into account.

Former French Prime Minister, Raymond Barre

They said, "You know, this issue doesn't seem to resignate with the people."
And I said, you know something? Whether it resignates or not doesn't matter
to me, because I stand for doing what's the right thing, and what the right
thing is hearing the voices of people who work.

George W. Bush, on This Morning, *1 November 2000*

A sheep in sheep's clothing.

Winston Churchill, describing British PM, Clement Atlee

He occasionally stumbled over the truth, but hastily picked himself up and
hurried on as if nothing had happened.

Winston Churchill, describing British PM, Stanley Baldwin

Dan Quayle (on a campaign stop): Who are you?
Woman: I'm your secret service agent.

" The Law is an Ass

"

You were there until the time you left. Is that true?

Attorney's question to a witness in the courtroom

Question: What was the first thing your husband said to you when he woke up
that morning?

Answer: He said, "Where am I, Cathy?"

Question: And why did that upset you?

Answer: My name is Susan.

Courtroom exchange between an attorney and a witness

Were you present when your picture was being taken?

Attorney's question to a witness

Now doctor, isn't it true that when a person dies in his sleep, he doesn't know
about it until the next morning?

Question posed to a witness by an attorney, reported in the
Massachusetts Bar Association Lawyers' Journal

Was it you or your younger brother who was killed in the war?

Attorney's question to a witness in the courtroom

Question: Do you know if your daughter has ever been involved in voodoo

or the occult?

Answer: We both do.

Question: Voodoo?

Answer: We do.

Question: You do?

Answer: Yes, voodoo.

Courtroom exchange between an attorney and a witness

Did he kill you?

Question to a witness on the stand in the courtroom

Question: You say the stairs went down to the basement?

Answer: Yes.

Question: And these stairs, did they go up also?

Exchange between an attorney and a witness in the courtroom.

Question: She had three children, right?

Answer: Yes.

Question: How many were boys?

Answer: None.

Question: Were there any girls?

Courtroom exchange between an attorney and a witness in the courtroom.

Attorney: Doctor, before you performed the autopsy, did you check for a pulse?

Witness: No.

Attorney: Did you check for blood pressure?

Witness: No.

Attorney: Did you check for breathing?

Witness: No.

Attorney: So then, is it possible that the patient was alive when you began the autopsy?

Witness: No.

Attorney: How can you be so sure, Doctor?

Witness: Because his brain was sitting on my desk in a jar.

Attorney: But could the patient still have been alive, nevertheless?

Witness: It is possible that he could have been alive and practicing law somewhere.

Courtroom exchange between an attorney and a witness,
as reported in the Massachusetts Bar Association Lawyers' Journal

How far apart were the vehicles at the time of the collision?

Question to a witness in the courtroom

Question: You went on a rather elaborate honeymoon, didn't you?

Answer: I went to Europe, sir.

Question: And you took your new wife?

Courtroom exchange between an attorney and a witness

Question: How was your first marriage terminated?

Answer: By death.

Question: And by whose death was it terminated?

Courtroom exchange between an attorney and a witness

Question: Were you acquainted with the deceased?

Answer: Yes, sir.

Question: Before or after he died?

Courtroom exchange between an attorney and a witness

Question: Do you recall the time that you examined the body?

Answer: The autopsy started around 8.30 pm.

Question: And Mr [name] was dead at the time?

Answer: No, he was sitting on the table wondering why I was doing an autopsy.

Courtroom exchange between an attorney and an expert witness with a particularly dry sense of humor

The youngest son, the twenty-year-old, how old is he?

Question to a witness in the courtroom

Question: Can you describe the individual?

Answer: He was about medium height and had a beard.

Question: Was this a male, or a female?

Courtroom exchange between an attorney and an expert witness

" Sports—
It's a cliché of two halves "

Football is an incredible game. Sometimes it's so incredible, it's unbelievable.

Tom Landry, former Dallas Cowboys coach

This is like *déjà vu* all over again.

Yogi Berra, baseball legend (former New York Yankee and Mets player and coach)—the comment is widely attributed to Berra, though others have since been found guilty of the same gaffe

When I said they'd scored two goals, of course I meant they'd scored one.

George Hamilton, Irish soccer commentator

We all get heavier as we get older because there's a lot more information in our heads.

Vlade Divac, basketball player for the Los Angeles Lakers

I was glad to see Italy win. All the guys on the team were Italians.

Tommy Lasorda, former Dodgers manager

You're next, big mouth.

Sonny Liston—somewhat foolishly—to Cassius Clay after defeating
Floyd Patterson in 1963. Muhammed Ali subsequently
gave Sonny Liston a drubbing

The batsman's Holding, the bowler's Willey.

Brian Johnston, reporting precisely what was happening during a cricket match
as—unfortunately for him—Michael Holding faced Peter Willey.
"Johnners," as he was affectionately known, once spent ten minutes collapsing
in giggles after a comment he made on Radio 4's otherwise very serious
Test Match Special

You can observe a lot just by watching.

Yogi Berra, baseball legend

The Americans sowed the seed, and now they have reaped the whirlwind.

Sebastian Coe, former Olympic medallist for middle-distance
running, turning his hand to commentary

We estimate, and this isn't an estimation, that Greta Waitz is 80 seconds behind.

David Coleman, BBC sports commentator, famous for his gaffes—
dubbed "Colemanballs" by satirical magazine Private Eye

That Michael Jackson is amazing! Three plays in two minutes!

Al Gore, commenting at a basketball game in which
Michael Jordan was playing

He must have made that before he died.

Yogi Berra, referring to a Steve McQueen movie

The word "genius" isn't applicable in football. A genius is a guy like Norman Einstein.

Joe Theisman, former NFL Washington Redskins quarterback and sports commentator (to be fair, Theisman did explain later that a former classmate had this name)

I would like to thank my parents—especially my father and mother.

Snatched phrase from golfer Greg Norman's winning speech at the 1983 World Matchplay championships

My favourite part was when the other team scored a football and then we came right back on the next play and scored a football too.

Kathleen Kennedy Townsend, Maryland Lt. Governor and member of the Kennedy clan, during the Super Bowl in 2001 (what she should have said was, "a touchdown")

Shearer could be at 100 per cent fitness . . . but not peak fitness.

Graham Taylor, ex-England manager

With eight minutes left, the game could be won in the next five or ten minutes.

Jimmy Armfield, radio commentator

Done, through, washed-up.

> *Verdict in the* Atlanta Constitution *on Jack Nicklaus; a week later,*
> *the "Golden Bear" won the 1986 US Masters championship*

A contract on a piece of paper, saying you want to leave, is like a piece of paper saying you want to leave.

> *John Hollins*

Our consistency's been all over the place.

> *Andy Hinchcliffe*

I can't really remember the names of the clubs that we went to.

> *Shaquille O'Neal, replying to an interviewer who had asked whether*
> *he had visited the Parthenon during his recent trip to Greece*

I want to thank you for making this day necessary.

> *Yogi Berra, commenting on Yogi Berra Appreciation Day*
> *in St. Louis in 1947*

I'm just a prawn in the game.

> *Brian London, English boxer*

We're going to turn this team around 360 degrees.

> *Jason Kidd, after his drafting to US basketball team*
> *the Dallas Mavericks*

You guys line up alphabetically by height.

Bill Peterson, Florida State football coach

I'm going to graduate on time, no matter how long it takes.

Rod Brookin, senior basketball player at the University of Pittsburgh

He is accelerating all the time. That last lap was run in 64 seconds and the one before in 62.

David Coleman, BBC sports commentator

I'd find the fellow who lost it, and if he was poor, I'd return it.

Yogi Berra, when asked what he would do if he found a million dollars

She won't win a game.

Fred Perry on Billie-Jean King before the tennis match against Bobby Riggs in 1973. (She did)

What will you do when you leave football, Jack—will you stay in football?

Stuart Hall, on Radio 5 Live

It's a drag having to wear socks during matches, because the tan, like, stops at the ankles. I can never get my skin, like, color coordinated.

Monica Seles

They [Rosenborg] have won 66 games, and they've scored in all of them.

Brian Moore, on ITV

I would not say he (David Ginola) is the best left winger in the Premiership, but there are none better.

Ron Atkinson, TV pundit

I want to keep fighting because it is the only think that keeps me out of hamburger joints. If I don't fight, I'll eat this planet.

George Foreman

An inch or two either side of the post and that would have been a goal.

Dave Bassett, speaking on Sky Sports

There's no doubt in my mind that if the race had been 46 laps instead of 45 it would have been a McLaren first and second. But it didn't, so it wasn't.

Murray Walker, motorsport commentator

I was saying the other day, how often the most vulnerable area for goalies is between their legs.

Andy Gray, on Sky Sports

If you don't know where you are going, you will wind up somewhere else.

Yogi Berra, baseball legend

If you can't stand the heat in the dressing room, get out of the kitchen.

Terry Venables, former England manager

I think I can win. I've got nothing better to do this weekend.

David Feherty before the 1994 Open Golf Championship (he lost)

And the line-up for the final of the Women's 400 metres hurdles includes three Russians, two East Germans, a Pole, a Swede and a Frenchman.

David Coleman, BBC sports commentator

You better cut the pizza in four pieces, because I'm not hungry enough to eat six.

Yogi Berra, New York baseball star

And it's Mansell . . . Mansell . . . Nigel Mansell!

Murray Walker, apoplectic with excitement while describing the 1990 Monaco Grand Prix—only to realize in a fit of apologies that viewers were actually watching Frenchman Alain Prost

If you can't imitate him, don't copy him.

Yogi Berra

He sliced the ball when he had it on a plate.

Ron Atkinson

Baseball is 90 per cent mental—the other half is physical.

Yogi Berra, baseball legend

I don't think he's ever lost a race at 200 metres, except at 400.

David Coleman, covering the 1992 Olympic Games

There's nobody fitter at his age, except maybe Raquel Welch.

Ron Atkinson, commenting on 39-year-old Gordon Strachan

I take a two-hour nap, from one o'clock to four.

Yogi Berra, baseball legend

He's very fast and if he gets a yard ahead of himself nobody will catch him.

Bobby Robson, another former England manager

The young Ralf Schumacher has been upstaged by the teenager, Jenson Button, who is twenty.

Murray Walker, motorsport commentator

If there's a pile-up there, they'll have to give some of the players artificial insemination.

Curt Cowdy, US football commentator

Merseyside derbies usually last 90 minutes and I'm sure today's won't be any different.

Trevor Booking, TV pundit

A nickel isn't worth a dime today.

Yogi Berra

It gets late early out there.

Yogi Berra, referring to the poor light conditions in left field at the stadium

And Arsenal now have plenty of time to dictate the last few seconds.

Peter Jones, radio commentator

Her time is about 4.33, which she's capable of.

David Coleman, sports commentator

. . . and so they have not been able to improve their 100 per cent record.

Sports Round-up

Batistuta is very good at pulling off defenders.

Kevin Keegan, yet another, former England manager

The girls in front are breaking wind.

Anonymous US commentator on the women's cycling event,
1984 Los Angeles Olympics

I'm going to make a prediction—it could go either way.

Ron Atkinson, TV pundit

If you come to a fork in the road, take it.

Yogi Berra, baseball legend

Thanks, you don't look so hot yourself.

Yogi Berra, after being told he looked cool

Strangely, in slow motion replay, the ball seemed to hang in the air for even
longer.

David Acfield

Slump? I ain't in no slump. I just ain't hitting.

Yogi Berra (the phrase was later taken up and paraphrased
by Dave Henderson, Oakland A's player)

Do my eyes deceive me or is Senna's car sounding a bit rough?

Murray Walker, motorsports commentator

There's only a second between them. One. That's how long a second is.

Murray Walker, motorsports commentator

The only thing I have in common with George Best is that we come from the
same place . . . play for the same club . . . and were discovered by the same
man.

Norman Whiteside

The Republic of China—back in the Olympic Games for the first time.

David Coleman, BBC sports commentator

They're the second best team in the world, and there's no higher praise than
that.

>>> *Kevin Keegan, when asked to comment on Argentina's qualities*

There goes Juantorena down the back straight, opening his legs and showing
his class.

>>> *David Coleman, commentating during the Montreal Olympics*

Yeah, but we're making great time!

>>> *Yogi Berra, in reply to, "Hey Yogi, I think we're lost"*

That's the fastest time ever run—but it's not as fast as the world record.

>>> *David Coleman, BBC sports commentator*

A mediocre season for Nelson Piquet, as he is now known, and always has been.

>>> *Murray Walker, motorsports commentator*

I've never had major knee surgery on any other part of my body.

>>> *Winston Bennett, former University of Kentucky basketball forward*

Me and George and Billy are two of a kind.

>>> *Micky Rivers, Texas Rangers outfielder, showing he can (not) count—*
>>> *while at the same time commenting on his warm relationship with Yankee*
>>> *owner Steinbrenner and manager Billy Martin*

Enos Cabell started out here with the Astros. And before that he was with the Orioles.

Jerry Coleman, San Diego Padres announcer

The wind always seems to blow against catchers when they are running.

Joe Garagiola

People think we make $3 million and $4 million a year. They don't realize that most of us only make $500,000.

Pete Incavigila, baseball player for the Texas Rangers

When your arm gets hit, the ball is not going to go where you want it to.

John Madden

Our offense is like the pythagorean theorem: There is no answer!

Shaquille O'Neal

Tambay's hopes, which were previously nil, are now absolutely zero.

Murray Walker, motorsports commentator

If you can't make the putts and can't get the man in from second on the bottom of the ninth, you're not going to win enough football games in this league, and that's the problem we had today.

Sam Rutigliano, coach for the Cleveland Browns, explaining in clear, multi-sport terms why his team had lost

And there's no damage to the car. Except to the car itself.

Murray Walker, motorsports commentator

A lot is said about defense, but at the end of the game, the team with the most points wins, the other team loses.

Isaiah Thomas, commentating on an NBA game.
(Bob Costas, obviously illuminated, replied, "Uh, well, OK")

I knew I was going to take the wrong train, so I left early.

Yogi Berra

This is an interesting circuit because it has inclines. And not just up, but down as well.

Murray Walker, motorsports commentator

Just under ten seconds . . . call it nine point five in round figures.

Murray Walker, motorsports commentator

Moses Kiptanui, the 19-year-old Kenyan, who turned 20 a few weeks ago.

David Coleman, sports commentator

It just as easily could have gone the other way.

Don Zimmer, Chicago Cubs manager, on his team's 4–4 record

Why buy good luggage? You only use it when you travel.

Yogi Berra, baseball legend

The par here at Sunningdale is 70 and anything under that will mean a score in
the sixties.

Steve Rider, numerically-sound golf presenter

If you'd offered me a 69 at the start this morning I'd have been all over you.

Sam Torrance, Ryder Cup golfer

It was impossible to get a conversation going; everybody was talking too much.

Yogi Berra

The lead car is absolutely unique—except for the car behind, which is identical.

Murray Walker, motorsports commentator

You give 100 per cent in the first half of the game, and if that isn't enough in the
second half you give what's left.

Yogi Berra

There's nothing wrong with the car except that it's on fire.

Murray Walker, motorsports commentator

We say, "educated left foot" . . . of course, there are many players with educated
right foots.

Ron Jones, on Radio 5 Live

Well, that was a cliff-dweller.

Wes Westrum, Mets coach, commentating on a close-run thing

In some respects, I do this to provoke people. I like experiencing people's reactions. Some people may take my message to be "sod off" and others an offer of sex. I am very aware of people's reactions and love the fact that people recognize me as Lars Elstrup.

Lars Elstrup, Ex-Denmark soccer player giving some useful
background information to explain his arrest for exposing himself in a
Copenhagen shopping center

Yes, it's true, I said "black shit" but he [Vieira] provoked me by saying "gypsy shit." I called him black but I might just as well have called him French . . . I didn't want to insult him because of the color of his skin just as I'm sure he didn't want to insult me by calling me a gypsy . . . I did call him "black bastard," but I didn't call him a monkey. He doesn't look like a monkey, but if he did I would probably have called him that.

Sinisa Mihajlovic, doing his bit to promote racial harmony
within European soccer

They were fourth division grounds but they haven't changed since they changed the name of the league, so they are, by definition, fourth division grounds.

Gabby Yorath, TV sports show host

One coach was training a player's hair, and another was training another part of his body.

Claudio Ranieri, commenting on Chelsea FC's training methods

If the fans don't come out to the ball park, you can't stop them.

Yogi Berra, baseball legend

He [Chris Coleman] swerved to avoid what he thinks was a deer. It all happened
so fast. He also said the animal could have been something smaller, like a
rabbit.

*Friend of Fulham player, Chris Coleman,
describing the accident that all but ended his playing career*

I'd say he's done more than that.

*Yogi Berra, when asked if first baseman Don Mattingly
had exceeded expectations for the current season*

The sight of opposing fans walking together down Wembley Way—you won't
get that anywhere other than Wembley.

John Sillett, soccer coach

I imagine the conditions in those cars are totally unimaginable.

Murray Walker, motorsports commentator

I was watching the Blackburn game on TV on Sunday when it flashed on the
screen that George [Ndah] had scored in the first minute at Birmingham. My
first reaction was to ring him up. Then I remembered he was out there
playing.

Ade Akinbiyi, fellow professional soccer player

I never heard a minute's silence like that.

> *Commentator, after a Wembley crowd had paid silent tribute*
> *to the late Diana, Princess of Wales*

One of the reasons Arnie (Arnold Palmer) is playing so well is that, before each tee shot, his wife takes out his balls and kisses them—Oh my God, what have I just said?

> *US golf commentator*

This is really a lovely horse. I once rode her mother.

> *Ted Walsh, racing commentator*

We now have exactly the same situation as we had at the start of the race, only exactly the opposite.

> *Murray Walker, motorsports commentator*

It's never happened in the World Series competition, and it still hasn't.

> *Yogi Berra, baseball legend*

The only problem I really have in the outfield is with flyballs.

> *Carmelo Martinez, San Diego Padres outfield player*

He dribbles a lot and the opposition don't like it—you can see it all over their faces.

> *Ron Atkinson, TV pundit*

How long have you known me, Jack? And you still don't know how to spell my
name.

Yogi Berra, upon receiving a cheque from Jack Buck made out to the "bearer"'
(the phrase is often repeated, and possibly apocryphal)

I couldn't settle in Italy. It was like being in a foreign country.

Ian Rush, commenting on the difficulties of adjusting to playing
soccer and living in a foreign country

Sure there have been injuries and deaths in boxing—but none of them serious.

Alan Minter, boxer

With the race half gone there is half the race still to go.

Murray Walker, motorsports commentator

The race course is as level as a billiard ball.

John Francombe, jockey

Ah, isn't that nice, the wife of the Cambridge president is kissing the cox of the
Oxford crew.

Harry Carpenter, commentating on the Oxford vs Cambridge Boat Race
on BBC TV in 1977

. . . and later we will have action from the men's cockless pairs.

Sue Barker, former tennis player, now a sports anchor

Here we are in the Holy Land of Israel—a Mecca for tourists.

> *David Vine, sports commentator—doing his bit to promote understanding of the*
> *geopolitical situation in the Middle East*

Morcelli has the four fastest 1500-meter times ever, and all those times at 1500 meters.

> *David Coleman, sports commentator*

Interviewer: "Have you ever thought of writing your autobiography?"
Chris Eubank (boxer): "On what?"

Sex is an anti-climax after that!

> *Mark Fitzgerald, Grand National-winning jockey*

These greens are so fast they must bikini-wax them.

> *Gary McCord, commenting on the pace of the greens at Augusta*

A sad ending, albeit a happy one.

> *Murray Walker, motorsports commentator*

Street hockey is great for kids. It's energetic, competitive and skilful. And best of all it keeps them off the street.

> *Snippet from UK radio news report*

It was the fastest-ever swim over that distance on American soil.

> *Greg Phillips*

I never blame myself when I'm not hitting. I just blame the bat, and if it keeps
up, I change bats. After all, if I know it isn't my fault that I'm not hitting, how
can I get mad at myself?

Yogi Berra, baseball legend

(There are) fears that the balloon may be forced to ditch in the Pacific. Mr
Branson, however, remains buoyant and hopes to reach America.

Radio 4 News

It ain't the heat; it's the humility.

Yogi Berra, baseball legend

The players returned to their respectable bases.

Dizzy Dean, baseball star

A fascinating duel between three men.

*David Coleman, sports commentator, describing the hammer throwing event
at the World Athletic Championships*

Winfield goes back to the wall. He hits his head on the wall and it rolls off! It's
rolling all the way back to second base! This is a terrible thing for the Padres!

Jerry Coleman, San Diego Padres announcer

Azinger is wearing an all-black outfit: black jumper, blue trousers, white shoes
and a pink "tea-cosy" hat.

Golf commentator Renton Laidlaw, displaying 20–20 color vision

The advantage of the rain is that if you have a quick bike, there's no advantage.

Barry Sheene, motorbike legend

Her legs are kept tightly together: she's giving nothing away.

Gymnastics commentator on BBC1

You should always go to other people's funerals; otherwise, they won't come to yours.

Yogi Berra, baseball legend

The tires are called wets, because they're used in the wet. And these tires are called slicks, because they're very slick.

Murray Walker, motorsports commentator

In cycling, you can put all your money on one horse.

Stephen Roche, Irish pro-cycler turned Eurosport commentator

It's amazing how, in this part of the world, history has been part of its past.

David Duffield, Tour de France commentator on Eurosport

Well, Burkhart's in the red—not only did he play it safely, he played it dangerously.

David Coleman, sports commentator

So, this movie you star in, *The Life Story of George Best*, tell us what it's about.

George Gavin, Sky Sports, interviewing soccer legend George Best

As Phil De Glanville said, each game is unique, and this one is no different to any other.

John Sleightholme, rugby commentator

And Prost can see Mansell in his earphones.

Murray Walker, motorsports commentator

They brought me up to the Brooklyn Dodgers, which at that time was in Brooklyn.

Casey Stengel, baseball legend

There you see Vicente Fernandez. He's limping because one leg is shorter than the rest.

Roddy Carr, commentating on the Irish Open golf tournament

You couldn't really find two more completely different personalities than these two men, Tom Watson and Brian Barnes; one is the complete golf professional and the other, the complete professional golfer.

Peter Alliss, doyen of golf commentators

Either that car is stationary or it is on the move!

Murray Walker, motorsports commentator

I would like to thank the press from the heart of my bottom.

Nick Faldo's winning speech after his 1992 Open championship

Fundamental Blunders—
From the mouth of babes
and those who should
know better

A fort is a place to put men in, and a fortress a place to put women in.

Schoolchild's attempt to explain the meaning of "fort" and "fortress"

Ousted RSPCA chief [Royal Society for the Prevention of Cruelty to Animals]
says he was a scapegoat.

Mention in The Times

Nitrogen is not found in Ireland because it is not found in a free state.

From an answer in a science exam

In Austria the principal occupation is gathering Austrich [sic] feathers.

Schoolroom blunder, nineteenth century

Heathen—from Latin *haethum*, faith, and *en*, not.

Schoolroom blunder, nonetheless displaying a flash of brilliance in attempting
to guess the etymology of a word

The Primate is the wife of the Prime Minister.

Schoolroom blunder, 1930s

Hey! They do Tudor over here too.

*American high school teacher to this author, during her days as a tour manager,
on first sighting of half-timbered buildings in Normandy*

The Puritans found an insane asylum in the wilds of America.

Schoolroom blunder, nineteenth century

Three kinds of blood vessels are; arteries, vanes and caterpillars.

From an answer in a science exam

Climate lasts all the time, and weather only a few days.

Schoolroom blunder, nineteenth century

A venerable gentleman with a long, grey board.

Misprint in The Times, *18 August 1871*

Question: What can you do to help ease a heavy traffic problem?

Answer: Carry loaded weapons.

*Real answer from an exam set by the California Department of Transportation's
driving school (for offending drivers . . .)*

When you breathe, you inspire. When you do not breathe, you expire.

From an answer in a science exam

A lifeboatman must possess great courage, a spirit of self-sacrifice and a
waterproof hat. He must not be selfish and grab the best seats. He should be
a sea dog to his last hair, and should possess a cheery mother, not one who
moans and groans, as it makes him miserable. Among little things a
lifeboatman should not have are wives or a child. Lifeboatmen have very red
noses because they get the very best fresh air. A lifeboatman should always
be prepared to give up his beauty sleep for others.

School essay, 1920s

Leap year is instead of it's being the next day on the same day next year, it's the
day after.

Schoolroom blunder, 1920s

To prevent contraception: wear a condominium.

From an answer in a science exam

A triangle with equal sides is called equatorial.

Schoolroom blunder, 1920s

Charles Darwin was a naturalist who wrote *The Organ of the Species*.

From a schoolchild's answer in a history exam, as reported by
Richard Lederer in his book, Anguished English

Handel was a quiet man, with twenty children. He was a German, but his father
suppressed his feelings.

Schoolroom blunder, 1920s

Sanscrit is not used as much as it used to be, as it went out of use 1500 BC.

Schoolroom blunder, nineteenth century

Transparent means, if you cannot see anything, it is not there.

Schoolroom blunder, 1930s

Blood flows down one leg and up the other.

From an answer in a science exam

The imports of a country are the things that are paid for; the exports are the things that are not.

Schoolboy's view of the economics of trade,
from an exam in the nineteenth century

He had a chronic disease—something the matter with the crone.

Schoolboy "diagnosis," nineteenth century

H_2O is hot water, and CO_2 is cold water.

From an answer in a science exam

The Britons were the Saxons who entered England in 1492 under Julius Caesar.

Extract from a schoolboy's history paper in the nineteenth century

We are sorry to announce that Mr Albert Brown has been quite unwell, owing to his recent death, and is taking a short holiday to recover.

Notice in a parish magazine

You break the law if you use mallet and forethought.

Schoolroom blunder, 1930s

For asphyxiation: Apply artificial respiration until the patient is dead.

From an answer in a science exam

He was the father of Lot, and had two wives. One was called Ishmale and the
other Hagher; he kept one at home, and he turned the other into the desert,
when she became a pillow of salt in the daytime and a pillow of fire at night.

Schoolchild's interpretation of the biblical story of Jonah, nineteenth century

The equator is a menagerie lion that walks around the middle of the earth.

Schoolroom blunder, 1920s

The Jacobites were famous for making biscuits.

Schoolroom blunder, 1930s

The moon is a planet just like the earth, only it is even deader.

From an answer in a science exam

Respiration is composed of two acts, first inspiration, and then expectoration.

From an answer in a science exam

Gorilla warfare is where men rode on gorillas.

Schoolroom blunder

Mosses [sic] was an Egyptian. He lived in an ark made of bullrushes, and he
kept a golden calf and worshipped braizen snakes, and et nothing but kwales
and manna for forty years. He was caught by the hair of his head, while riding
under the bough of a tree, and he was killed by his son, Absalom, as he was
hanging from the bough.

*Child's interpretation of the biblical story of
Moses—confusing wildly-different events*

Your medical assistance is cancelled beginning 9/24/84 because of your death.

Extract from a letter from the Iowa Department of Human Services

Cuba is a town in Africa very difficult of access.

Schoolroom blunder

Samuel Morse invented a code of telepathy.

*From a schoolchild's answer in a history exam, as reported by
Richard Lederer in his book,* Anguished English

Elijah was a good man, who went up to heaven without dying, and threw his
cloak down for Queen Elizabeth to step over.

*Schoolboy interpretation of the biblical story of Elijah—confusing events and
also spanning a huge space of time*

(Gibraltar is) an island built on a rock.

Schoolroom blunder

Question: Do you yield when a blind pedestrian is crossing the road?

Answer: What for? He can't see my license plate.

> *Real answer from exam set by the California Department of Transportation's*
> *driving school (for offending drivers . . .)*

She (Queen Mary) was wilful as a girl and cruel as a woman, but what can you expect from anyone who had had five stepmothers?

> *Schoolchild's history paper, from the nineteenth century*

In 1620 the Pilgrim Fathers made flowers (Mayflower) in the New England colony.

> *Schoolroom blunder, 1930s*

A magnetic force is a straight line, generally a curved one, which would tend to point to where the North Pole comes.

> *Schoolroom blunder, 1920s*

Artifical [sic] insemination is when the farmer does it to the cow instead of the bull.

> *From an answer in a science exam*

Letters in sloping types are in hysterics.

> *Schoolroom blunder, 1930s*

For head cold: use an agonizer to spray the nose until it drops in your throat.

> *From an answer in a science exam*

Ancient Egypt was inhabited by mummies, and they all wrote in hydraulics.
They lived in the Sarah Dessert and travelled by camelot. The climate of the
Sarah is such that the inhabitants have to live elsewhere, so certain areas of
the dessert are cultivated by irritation.

Examination paper gaffe, as reported by Richard Lederer
in his book, Anguished English

Question: Explain why, in order to cook food by boiling, at the top of a high
mountain, you must employ a different method from that used at the sea
level.
Answer: It is easy to cook food at the sea level by boiling it, but once you get
above the seal level the only plan is to fry it in its own fat. It is, in fact,
impossible to boil water above the sea level by any amount of heat. A
different method, therefore, would have to be employed to boil food at the top
of a high mountain, but what that method is has not yet been discovered. The
future may reveal it to a daring experimentalist.

Question and answer in an Acoustics, Light and Heat paper set by the Science
and Art Department, South Kensington, London, 1880

Dew is formed on leaves when the sun shines down on them and makes them
perspire.

From an answer in a science exam

The soil is fertile, because it is full of micro-orgasms.

Thirteen-year-old pupil at Cranleigh School, cutting sent in to
Quote Unquote *programme on BBC Radio 4*

151

The procession was very fine, and nearly two miles in length, as was also the
sermon of the minister.

Printed report in The New York Times *in 1855 of the funeral of*
William Poole in New York

A super-saturated solution is one that holds more than it can hold.

From an answer in a science exam

Gravity was invented by Isaac Walton. It is chiefly noticeable in the autumn,
when the apples are falling off the trees.

From a schoolchild's answer in a science exam, as reported by
Richard Lederer in his book, Anguished English

When you smell an oderless [sic] gas, it is probably carbon monoxide.

From an answer in a science exam

Isosceles triangles are used on maps to join up places that have the same
weather.

Schoolroom blunder, 1920s

We apologize for the error in last week's paper in which we stated that Mr
Arnold Dogbody was a defective in the police force. We meant, of course, that
Mr Dogbody is a detective in the police farce.

Correction notice in the Ely Standard, *Cambridgeshire, England*

Question: Explain why water pipes burst in cold weather.

Answer: People who have not studied acoustics think that Thor bursts the pipes, but we know that it is nothing of the kind for Professor Tyndall has burst the mythologies and has taught us that it is the natural behavior of water (and bismuth) without which all fish would die and the earth be held in an iron grip.

Question and answer in an Acoustics, Light and Heat paper set by the Science and Art Department, South Kensington, London, 1881

Gravity is seriousness. If it were to cease, we should all die of laughing.

Schoolroom blunder, 1920s

Question: What changes would occur in your lifestyle if you could no longer drive lawfully?

Answer: I would be forced to drive unlawfully.

Real answer from an exam set by the California Department of Transportation's driving school (for offending drivers . . .)

To collect fumes of sulphur, hold a deacon over a flame in a test tube.

From an answer in a science exam

Joan of Arc was burned to a steak.

From a schoolchild's answer in a history exam

Mushrooms always grow in damp places and so they look like umbrellas.

From an answer in a science exam

Louis Pasteur discovered a cure for rabbis.

> *From a schoolchild's answer in a history exam, as reported by Richard Lederer*
> *in his book,* Anguished English

The disciples put Jesus's body into a cave and rolled a rock across because they didn't want it to smell. Also, it stopped the wolves coming in and eating it. When they came and saw the rock had been rolled away, they knew a wolf couldn't have done it all by itself.

> *Contemporary junior high account of Jesus rising from the dead*

Erratum: The word "ambiguity" in our second leading article yesterday, should have been "anti-guity."

> *The* Natal Mercury, *22 June 1883, correcting an article from the previous day in which mention had been made of the world's "wonted tokens of ambiguity." The day afterwards,the following appeared in the paper: "Double Erratum: The unknown word 'anti-guity' in a local paragraph yesterday professing to correct the word 'ambiguity', should have been 'antiquity'"*

The letter X is very useful in algebra, because you can put it in when you cannot work out the sum.

> *Schoolroom blunder*

Bach was the most famous composer in the world, and so was Handle [sic]. Handle was half-German, half-Italian, and half-English. He was very large. Bach died from 1750 to the present.

> *From a schoolchild's answer in an exam*

The pilgrims went to Canterbury to kill Joe Beckett.

Schoolroom blunder, 1930s

The word "trousers" is an uncommon noun, because it is singular at the top and plural at the bottom.

Contemporary blunder

The tides are a fight between the earth and moon. All water tends towards the moon, because there is no water in the moon, and nature abhors a vacuum. I forget where the sun joins in this fight.

From an answer in a science exam

The dome of St Paul's is supported by eight peers. Unfortunately, they are cracked.

Schoolroom blunder, 1920s

Some people say we condescended from apes.

Contemporary schoolchild's blunder

To keep milk from turning sour, keep it in the cow.

From answer in a science exam

Water freezes at 32 degrees and boils at 212 degrees. There are 180 degrees between freezing and boiling because there are 180 degrees between north and south.

Contemporary schoolchild's blunder

The Greeks were a highly sculptured people, and without them we wouldn't have history. The Greeks invented three kinds of columns—corinthian, ironic, and doric—and built the Apocalypse. The Greeks also had myths. A myth is a female moth.

Examination paper gaffe, as reported by Richard Lederer in his book, Anguished English

The function of the skin is to keep in the bones, and we look much nicer with the skin on. If we had no skin we should go about skeletons.

Schoolroom blunder, 1920s

The earth makes a resolution every 24 hours.

Contemporary schoolchild's howler

The pistol of a flower is its only protection against insects.

From an answer in a science exam

Raleigh died in James I's reign and started smoking.

Schoolroom blunder, 1920s

The dodo is a bird that is nearly decent now.

Junior high mistake

Alfred the Great conquered the Dames.

From a schoolchild's answer in a history exam, as reported by Richard Lederer in his book, Anguished English

The alimentary canal is located in the northern part of Indiana.

From an answer in a science exam

Geometry teaches us to bisex angels.

Junior high student's error

King Harold mustarded his troops before the Battle of Hastings.

From a schoolchild's answer in a history exam, as reported by
Richard Lederer in his book, Anguished English

One of the main causes of dust is janitors.

Junior high student's error

The skeleton is what is left after the insides have been taken out and the
outsides have been taken off. The purpose of the skeleton is something to
hitch meat to.

From an answer in a science exam

The Wizard of the North was Mr Lloyd George. He is a hard-working libel.

Schoolboy error, 1920s (referring to the former Liberal Prime Minister)

The slag floats on the iron because they have different dentists.

Contemporary GCSE student, writing about the blast furnace

An axiom is a thing which is so visible that it is not necessary to see it.

Schoolroom blunder, 1920s

Writing at the same time as Shakespeare was Miguel Cervantes. He wrote
Donkey Hote (*Don Quixote*).

> *From a schoolchild's answer in an English exam, as reported by*
> *Richard Lederer in his book,* Anguished English

The laws of chemical union are like the laws of any other union, pretty strict,
and have a lot to dowith blacklegs.

> *Schoolroom blunder, 1920s*

Many women belive [sic] that an alcoholic binge will have no ill-effects on the
unborn fetus, but that is a large misconception.

> *From an answer in a science exam*

It is so hot in some places that people there have to live in other places.

> *Contemporary schoolroom blunder*

Acrimony, which is sometimes called holy, is another name for marriage.

> *Schoolroom blunder, 1920s*

A permanent set of teeth consists of eight canines, eight cuspids, two molars,
and eight cuspidors.

> *From an answer in a science exam*

Water is composed of two gins, Oxygin and Hydrogin. Oxygin is pure gin, and
Hydrogin is gin and water.

> *Schoolroom blunder, 1920s*

A fossil is an extinct animal. The older it is, the more extinct it is.

From an answer in a science exam

Robinson Crusoe was the first Roman leader to come to our country. Feeling very miserable he looked for food. Soon he began to feel an emptyness in his neck, but it was no use. Then he saw Friday coming to him with a handful of coconuts.

Schoolroom blunder, 1920s

King John lost all of his clothes in the wash and afterwards died of shock.

Schoolroom blunder, 1920s

Germinate: To become a naturalized German.

From an answer in a science exam

God tried Abraham by giving him a wife and children.

Schoolroom blunder, 1920s

A lot of Englishmen were shut up in the black hole of Calcutta with one small widow. Only four got out alive.

Schoolroom blunder, 1920s

. . . to install a component into the structural fabric.

Extract from a document for a bricklaying NVQ (National Vocational Qualification)—the above simply describes the action of placing a brick in a wall.
As reported by the Plain English Campaign

Litter: A nest of young puppies.

From an answer in a science exam

Magnet: Something you find crawling all over a dead cat.

From an answer in a science exam

And you, you brute.

Schoolchild's translation, from Latin, of "Et tu Brute," the dying words of the Roman emperor Julius Caesar (they should have been translated as, "You also, Brutus?")

Momentum: What you give a person when they are going away.

From an answer in a science exam

Gargoyles are often seen on people's necks.

Schoolroom blunder, 1920s

SOTP

Painted instruction on a road—the misspelt "STOP" marking was photographed and sent into Knowtypos, (knowtypos.com), where editorial accuracy is prized, and there placed in their "Hall of Shame"

Due to a typing error, Gov. Dukakis was incorrectly identified in the third paragraph as Mike Tyson.

Correction printed in a Massachusetts newspaper

Entry Level: The acquisition of a limited range of basic skills, knowledge and understanding in highly structured and self-referenced contexts which permit the identification of progression from the learner's point of entry to the learning process.

Extract from a night student's "Credit Record" folder, from the Open College Network. As reported by the Plain English Campaign

Planet: A body of earth surrounded by sky.

From an answer in a science exam

A blizzard is the inside of a duck.

Schoolroom blunder, 1920s

Rhubarb: A kind of celery gone bloodshot.

From an answer in a science exam.

Please provide the date of your death.

Letter from the IRS

The greatest writer of the futile ages was Chaucer, who wrote many poems and verses and also wrote literature.

From a schoolchild's answer in an English exam, as reported by Richard Lederer in his book, Anguished English

Vacuum: A large, empty space where the pope lives.

From an answer in a science exam

Meccano was the name of a famous Italian statesman.

Schoolroom blunder, 1930s

Evolution is what Darwin did. Devolution is something to do with Satan.

*Schoolchild's error, 1920s (though some British Conservatives of the 1980s
might have agreed with the latter statement)*

Question: Who has the right of way when four cars approach a four-way stop at
the same time?
Answer: The pick-up truck with the gun rack and the bumper sticker
saying, "Guns don't kill people, I do."

*Real answer from exam set by the California Department of Transportation's
driving school (for offending drivers . . .)*

Before giving a blood transfusion, find out if the blood is affirmative or negative.

From an answer in a science exam

To remove dust from the eye, pull the eye down over the nose.

From an answer in a science exam

For dog bite: put the dog away for several days. If he has not recovered,
then kill it.

From an answer in a science exam

For a nosebleed: Put the nose much lower then the body until the heart stops.

From an answer in a science exam

The Florence Nightingale was born in the year 1855, the year of the Crimean War. It always used to warn the English if the enemy was near. In this way it used to fly about from place to place, and then when it saw them it would fly back to the English and make an officer look and lead the way. It died in the year 1906. The result is we have now what are called messenger birds, that is that people take a pigeon and pin a letter under its wing and on its leg they put a silver or leather ring.

School essay, 1920s, (a time when sherbet was clearly a mind-altering substance)

A former Chichester Diocesan Moral Welfare Secretary was trained at Josephine Butler House, Liverpool, and spent much of her time in this diocese under Bishop Bell.

Career move noted in parish magazine

A number of deaths unavoidably postponed.

Heading in the "Births, Marriages and Deaths" column of a local newspaper in the late nineteenth century–slipped in by a sub-editor in a hurry

Mr Gladstone as a Farce.

Headline in a political article in the Pall Mall Gazette, *1880s (the sentiment of the article strongly suggested that the "a" should have been an "o")*

Culture—
and its vultures

All my shows are great. Some of them are bad. But they are all great.

Sir Lew Grade, film producer, September 1975

Come here quick. There's something that will make you laugh.

King George V to his wife, Queen Mary, on coming across an exhibition
of French Impressionist paintings during a royal visit to the
Tate Gallery, London

I tell you, cocaine isn't habit forming. I know, because I've been taking it for
years.

Tallulah Bankhead

Beautiful, my dear Mozart, but too many notes.

Emperor Joseph II, something of a musical dilettante, giving the benefit of his
musical "advice" to Mozart after a performance of the opera
The Abduction from the Seraglio

Can't act, can't sing, balding slightly . . . Can dance a little.

MGM talent scout, on aspiring hopeful Fred Astaire in 1928

How can we sit together and deal with this industry if you're going to do things like that to me? If this is the way you do it, gentlemen, include me out.

Hollywood producer Samuel Goldwyn, regarding a labor dispute with Jack L. Warner over Busby Berkeley ("include me out" was one of the many so-called "Goldwynisms"–real or attributed–for which the movie mogul became known)

I'm going to be bigger than The Beatles.

Crispian St Peters (now a total unknown) in 1966

Within the veracity of geography and the resonance of history, the Museum of Scotland offers a lexicon of spatial types to suit the collection's variety of objects, artificially locating them within a recognizable domain. Circulation occupies a liminal zone, offering a contrapuntal journey beyond the taxonomy of collections or chronology.

Snippet from article by Gordon Benson in the Architectural Review—
featured in "Pseuds' Corner" of Private Eye

I must be the luckiest man in the world. Not only am I bisexual, I am also Welsh.

John Osborne, playwright

I never knew a guitar player worth a damn.

Vernon Presley, to his young son Elvis, in 1954

In my opinion, she's nix.

Howard Hughes, director, on actress Jean Harlow, who was then still called Harlean Carpenter (his opinion was shared by screenwriter Joseph March, who declared, "My God, she's got a shape like a dustpan")

Kinquering Congs their titles take.

Rev. William Archibald Spooner (1844–1930), Warden of New College, Oxford, announcing the hymn in New College Chapel. Spooner was renowned for his habit of transposing the initial sounds, and other parts, of two or more words— the phrases this produced thus became known as "spoonerisms"

Very sorry can't come. Lie follows by post.

Baron Beresford (Charles William de la Poer, 1846–1919), British naval officer and author of A Life of Nelson, *replying by telegram to an eleventh-hour dinner invitation from Edward, Prince of Wales*

You're not the acting type.

Headmaster of Pembroke Lodge School to a certain schoolboy by the name of Alec Guinness

Yet it is better to drop thy friends, O my daughter, than to drop thy "H's."

C.S. Calverley, British poet (d. 1884)

I'm conducting slowly because I don't know the tempo.

Eugene Ormandy, conductor and music director
of the Philadelphia Orchestra

(He) converted ten thousand persons on a desert island.

Sentence from an early record of the life of St Francis Xavier, written by an
Italian monk (recorded in Bulls, Blunders and Howlers, *1928)*

If you live to the age of a hundred, you have it made, because very few people
die past the age of a hundred.

George Burns

Put it out of your mind. In no time, it will be a forgotten memory.

Samuel Goldwyn, Hollywood producer

His ears make him look like a taxicab with both doors open.

Howard Hughes, director, passing judgement on Clark Gable

Oh, really? What exactly is she reading?

Dame Edith Evans, on being told that writer Nancy Mitford
had been lent a villa so that she could finish her book

You ought to hear Claud play *Kitten on the Keys*.

Hushed whisper by member of the audience at a Beethoven concert, overheard
by W. Leslie Nicholls (sent in to the New Statesman*)*

Am in Market Harborough. Where ought I to be?

G.K. Chesterton (1874–1936), writer, in a telegram to his wife.
Chesterton was notorious for his lack of organization

Adolf Hitler was a Jeanne d'Arc, a saint. He was a martyr. Like many martyrs,
he held extreme views.

Ezra Pound, in an interview in the US on 9 May 1945

Going to call him "William?" What kind of a name is that? Every Tom, Dick and
Harry's called William. Why don't you call him "Bill?"

Samuel Goldwyn, Hollywood producer

Regret the American public is not interested in anything on China.

Rejection note to Pearl Buck, 1931, regarding the manuscript
for The Good Earth

Thou shalt commit adultery.

The Seventh Commandment, as printed in the 1632 edition of the Bible
(the printers were fined 300 pounds for their error—a sum sufficient
to put them out of business)

(To an undergraduate) Sir, you have tasted two whole worms.

Rev. William Archibald Spooner, (he meant, "wasted two whole terms")

We must believe in free will. We have no choice.

Isaac Bashevis, singer

For your information, just answer me one question!

Samuel Goldwyn

I think it is only a matter of time before you reach out into more substantial efforts that will be capable of making some real money in books.

Rejection letter to James M. Cain, author of The Postman Always Rings Twice, *which subsequently became a major Hollywood film*

Actors, like the doctors in Chekhov, are often consumed by a sense of having betrayed their own calling, of having disappointed themselves and God; the dachas in which so many of the plays take place are like so many green rooms.

Simon Callow, actor, originally quoted in The Guardian *newspaper– entry sent into "Luvvies' Corner" of* Private Eye

(To an Oxford undergraduate) You have hissed all my mystery lectures.

Rev. William Archibald Spooner, (he meant, "missed all my history lectures")

It does not seem to us that you have been wholly successful in working out an admittedly promising idea.

Rejection letter to William Golding for Lord of the Flies, *1954*

Yes, but that's our strongest weak point.

Samuel Goldwyn, when asked early in his career whether he'd ever made a picture

Rock and roll is phony and false. And it's sung, written and played for the most part by cretinous goons.

Frank Sinatra, in 1957

As long as the plots keep coming from outer space, I'll keep going on with my virgins.

Barbara Cartland

He hasn't got any future.

Rejection letter to John Le Carré, author of
The Spy Who Came in From the Cold *and* Smiley's People

I guess you thought I was conducting, but I wasn't.

Eugene Ormandy, conductor and music director of the Philadelphia Orchestra

Experience teaches us two things: the first, that one must correct endlessly; the second, that one must not correct excessively.

Eugene Delacroix, French painter

If I look confused it's because I'm thinking.

Samuel Goldwyn

Color and stereoscopy will make the cinema into the greatest art in the world. Bad films will be impossible.

Sir John Betjeman, Poet Laureate

I am thinking it right . . . but beating it wrong.

Eugene Ormandy, conductor and music director of the Philadelphia Orchestra

I remember your name perfectly, but I've completely forgotten your face.

Rev. William Spooner

Television has brought back murder into the home—where it belongs.

Alfred Hitchcock, December 1965

He treats me like the dirt under my feet.

Samuel Goldwyn

We counsel him to forthwith abandon poetry . . .

The Edinburgh Review *on Lord Byron's early work*

The ideal voice for radio should have no substance, no sex, no owner, and a
message of importance for every housewife.

Ed Murrow, 1 May 1949

I told him he'd have a heart attack a year ago, but unfortunately he lived a year
longer.

Eugene Ormandy, on the death of David Oistrakh

So you realize, young woman, that you're the first American writer ever to poke
fun at sex?

Rejection note to Anita Loos, 1925, author of Gentlemen Prefer Blondes

You will leave Oxford by the next town drain.

Rev. William Archibald Spooner, upon dismissing an undergraduate

To hell with the cost, if it's a good story, I'll make it.

Samuel Goldwyn, on being told that the script
then under consideration was "too caustic"

It will not sell, and it will do immeasurable harm to a growing reputation . . . I recommend that it be buried under a stone for a thousand years.

Rejection letter to Vladimir Nabokov in 1955 for his novel Lolita

When the boys come back from France, we'll have the hags flung out.

Rev. William Archibald Spooner, (he meant, "flags hung out")

I'll have to see him before I believe he's invisible.

Line from the film The Invisible Man Returns, *1940*

I paused when I came to the name of the hero, "Rhett Butler." Undiscouraged, I pressed on. But when I came to the name of the heroine, "Scarlett O'Hara," I dropped the whole matter. I had no intention of getting mixed up in another version of *Terry and the Pirates* and *The Dragon Lady and Lace.*

Nunnally Johnson, screenwriter for 20th Century Fox, on his negative
impressions from looking over the synopsis submitted for the film version of
Gone With The Wind. *As quoted in* Don't Quote Me, *by Don Atyeo and*
Jonathan Green, 1981

We have all passed a lot of water since then.

Samuel Goldwyn

This fictional account of the day-by-day life of an English gamekeeper is still of
considerable interest to outdoor-minded readers, as it contains many
passages on pheasant raising, the apprehending of poachers, ways to control
vermin, and other chores and duties of the professional gamekeeper.
Unfortunately one is obliged to wade through many passages of extraneous
material in order to discover and savor these sidelights on the management of
a Midlands shooting estate, and in this reviewer's opinion, this book cannot
take the place of J.R. Miller's Practical Gamekeeping.

Anonymous review of D.H. Lawrence's Lady Chatterley's Lover,
attributed to Field and Stream, *c. 1928*

They are doomed to an early and expensive death.

A.P. Herbert, writer for London-based Punch *magazine,
forecasting an end to talking films*

The girl (Ann Frank) doesn't, it seems to me, have a special perception or feeling
which would lift that book above the curiosity level.

Rejection note for The Diary of Anne Frank, *1952*

I keep my icicle well boiled.

*Rev. William Archibald Spooner, (he meant, "bicycle well oiled."
Also recorded as, "Give me a well-boiled icicle")*

I never read any novels except my own. When I feel worried, agitated or upset, I read one and find the last pages soothe me and leave me happy. I quite understand why I am popular in hospitals.

Barbara Cartland

Don't send them. They're so bad, they'll spoil it for the others.
Leader of the band, Howie Casey and the Seniors, pleading from Hamburg, Germany, with The Beatles' agent

It is impossible that it could be true and therefore it is without real value.
Rejection letter to Herman Melville for his novel Typee, *1846*

I have been laid up with intentional flu.

Samuel Goldwyn

Such was Catherine Morland at ten. At fifteen, appearances were mending; she began to cut her hair and long for balls . . .
Jane Austen, from the novel Northanger Abbey *(with apologies to one of the finest writers England has produced)*

I am still an atheist, thank God.

Luis Buñuel, Spanish film director

My dear sir,
I have read your manuscript. Oh, my dear sir.
Rejection letter to Oscar Wilde, 1892, for his play Lady Windermere's Fan

It is impossible to sell animal stories in the U.S.A . . . I think the choice of pigs as the ruling caste will no doubt give offense to many people, and particularly to anyone who is a bit touchy, as undoubtedly the Russians are . . .

Rejection letter to George Orwell in 1945
for his manuscript for Animal Farm

I'm willing to admit that I may not always be right, but I am never wrong.

Samuel Goldwyn

The opening line contains too many 'r's.

Rejection letter to Ezra Pound, 1912, for Portrait d'Une Femme

If Beethoven's *Seventh Symphony* is not by some means abridged, it will soon fall into disuse.

Philip Hale, Boston music critic, in 1837

My dear fellow, I may be dead from the neck up, but rack my brains as I may, I can't see why a chap should need thirty pages to describe how he turns over in bed before going to sleep.

Rejection letter to Marcel Proust for Swann's Way
(one volume in the series Remembrance of Things Past*)*

When he lost the game, he received a blushing crow.

Reverend William Archibald Spooner,
(he meant, "a crushing blow")

They stayed away in droves.

Samuel Goldwyn

To be frank, Mr Epstein, we don't like your boys' sound . . . Groups of guitarists
are on the way out.

Decca Records boss Dick Rowe, rejecting The Beatles in 1962

I'm just glad it'll be Clark Gable who's falling on his face and not Gary Cooper.

*Gary Cooper on his decision not to take the leading role
in the film* Gone With the Wind

A long, dull novel about an artist.

Rejection letter in 1934 to Irving Stone for Lust for Life, *Stone's
fictional biography of painter Vincent Van Gogh. The book went
on to sell 25 million copies*

A verbal contract is not worth the paper it's written on.

Samuel Goldwyn

Who the hell wants to hear actors talk?

*H.M. Warner, Warner Brothers, ruling out the popularity
of the talkies in 1927*

We don't think The Beatles will do anything in this market.

Jay Livingstone, head of America's Capitol Records, in 1964

Too slow . . . confusing and irritating . . . issues too clear-cut and old-fashioned.

Some of the comments from the numerous publishing houses to have rejected Frank Herbert's manuscript, Dune *(once published, it went on to sell ten million copies worldwide)*

Don't improve it into a flop!

Samuel Goldwyn

I am one hundred per cent certain that Hitler wrote every single word in those books . . . (It's) the journalistic scoop of the post-World War II period.

Peter Koch, editor of Stern *magazine, April 1983 (the German magazine had announced that they had gained possession of Adolf Hitler's secret diaries—all 62 volumes. Later in the same year, it was proved the diaries had been faked)*

Mr Lawrence has a diseased mind. He is obsessed by sex and we have no doubt that he will be ostracized by all except the most degenerate coteries of the world.

The British John Bull *magazine, on* Lady Chatterley's Lover *in 1928*

The African killer bee portrayed in this film bears absolutely no relationship to the industrious, hard-working American honeybee to which we are indebted for pollinating vital crops that feed our nation.

Notice at the end of the film The Swarm *(1978)—just in case anyone was thinking otherwise, and to ensure the American bee's reputation remained untainted by the despicable behavior of its naughty relations in the film*

Let us glase our asses and toast the queer old Dean.

> *Rev. William Archibald Spooner, proposing a toast to Queen Victoria,*
> *(also recorded as, "Gentlemen, raise your glasses to the queer old dean")*

Nothing but a pack of lies.

> *Damon Runyon, passing judgement on* Alice in Wonderland *by Lewis Carroll*

I wouldn't be able to sell ten copies.

> *Rejection note to the French writer Colette,*
> *for her manuscript* Claudine in School, *c.1900*

Let me sew you to your sheet.

> *Rev. William Archibald Spooner, (he meant, "show you to your seat")*

True, I've been a long time making up my mind, but now I'm giving you a definite answer. I won't say yes, and I won't say no—but I'm giving you a definite maybe.

> *Samuel Goldwyn*

He's *passé*. Nobody cares about Mickey any more. There are whole batches of Mickeys we just can't give away. I think we should phase him out.

> *Roy Disney (brother of Walt), in the 1930s*

(For) fear people would laugh.

> *Explanation given by the conductor who had decided to skip part of the*
> *last movement of Beethoven's* First Symphony *in 1801*

Come on Kong, forget about me. The thing's just never going to work, can't you see?

> *Line spoken by the actress Jessica Lange, to King Kong,*
> *in the film of the same name from 1976*

Rembrandt is not to be compared in the painting of character with our extraordinarily gifted artist, Mr Rippingille.

> *John Hunt, British art critic, dismissing the famous Dutch artist*
> *in favour of a, now, complete unknown from the early 1800s*

Bizet was a very young man when he composed this symphony, so play it soft.

> *Eugene Ormandy, conductor and music director of the Philadelphia Orchestra*

You'll sink, not like a lead balloon, but even faster, like a lead zeppelin.

> *Keith Moon, drummer with The Who, to guitarist Jimmy Page,*
> *on the future of the group Page was planning to form—*
> *they became, thanks to this out-of-hand dismissal, Led Zeppelin*

If I could have had that girl's body, even with my wife's head, I would have been a happier man.

> *The Duke of Urbino, sixteenth-century ruler, to Pietro Aretino, Italian satirist,*
> *and the painter Titian, who had been asked to paint a nude portrait of the old*
> *and ugly duchess, his wife. (Aretino had made the suggestion to hire a beautiful*
> *young prostitute to provide the "body," and the result—the Venus of Urbino—as*
> *recorded above, was pleasing to the duke.) However, Aretino found the remark*
> *so hilarious that he had a laughing fit that led to a fatal stroke*

Reagan doesn't have the presidential look.

> *Executive from United Artists, giving young actor Ronald Reagan the thumbs down for the leading role in the film* The Best Man, *1964*

Every director bites the hand that lays the golden egg.

> *Samuel Goldwyn*

One who scatters cholera germs is less of a menace to society than one who sells an impure book.

> *E. Tallmadge Root, one of Boston's religious leaders regarding D. H. Lawrence's novel* Lady Chatterley's Lover *going on sale in that city in the 1920s*

Twelve? So who needs twelve? Couldn't we make do with six?

> *Lew Grade, film producer, on being told by Franco Zeffirelli, his director, that the budget for the film* Jesus of Nazareth *simply had to stretch to twelve disciples*

Why only twelve disciples? Go out and get thousands!

> *Samuel Goldwyn*

Tell them to stand closer apart.

> *Samuel Goldwyn*

You ain't goin' nowhere, son. You ought to go back to drivin' a truck.

> *Jim Denny of the Grand Ole Opry, Nashville, firing Elvis Presley after his first performance, 1954*

You may think that one of the ways in which you can test this book, and test it from the most liberal outlook, is to ask yourselves the question, when you have read it through, would you approve of your young sons, young daughters—because girls can read as well as boys—reading this book. Is it a book that you would have lying around in your own house? Is it a book that you would even wish your wife or your servants to read?

Mervyn Griffith-Jones to the jury at the Old Bailey in October 1960, on the question of whether Penguin Books should be allowed to publish an unexpurgated edition of D.H. Lawrence's Lady Chatterley's Lover. *His outdated —and somewhat patronizing—approach provoked amusement in the courtroom and the country at large*

Damien Hirst tends to use everyday objects such as a shark in formaldehyde.

Arts Commentator, BBC Radio 4

I don't want yes-men around me. I want everyone to tell the truth, even if it costs them their jobs.

Samuel Goldwyn

It gives me the hydrostatics to such a degree.

Mrs Malaprop, a character in the play The Rivals *(1775), by Richard Brinsley Sheridan*

If you're not pretty and you're working class, you have an easier time.

Helena Bonham-Carter, actress, quoted in the Independent on Sunday, *"Quotes of the Week," October 1996*

Yes, but keep copies.

> *Samuel Goldwyn, when asked by his secretary whether*
> *she should destroy files which were over ten years old*

At every concert I've sensed a certain insecurity about the tempo. It's clearly marked 80 . . . uh, 69.

> *Eugene Ormandy, conductor and music director of the Philadelphia Orchestra*

If there is a meaning (in this film), it is doubtless objectionable.

> *Comment by British Board of Film Censors, banning Jean Cocteau's film*
> The Seashell and the Clergyman *(1929)*

I don't think anyone should write his autobiography until after he's dead.

> *Samuel Goldwyn*

What can you do with a guy with ears like that?

> *Jack Warner, movie mogul, rejecting Clark Gable, 1930*

In two words, impossible.

> *Samuel Goldwyn*

Nice of you to come, but your head's too small for the camera, you are too thin, and . . . I don't know what it is exactly about the neck . . . but it's not right.

> *Studio executive Earl St. John to English actor Dirk Bogarde,*
> *who was auditioning at Rank Organization. Quoted in* Snakes and Ladders,
> *by Dirk Bogarde, 1978*

Try another profession. Any other.

Head of New York's John Murray Anderson Drama School,
to a youthful Lucille Ball

Never will Betty Bacall attain a caviar and champagne lifestyle.

Walter Thornton, model agency boss, talking about Lauren Bacall
(later to become a hugely successful Hollywood actress and to
marry Humphrey Bogart)

The talking picture is like a dress rehearsal in the theatre. It never gets those
moments of inspiration when an audience lifts an actor out of himself. So I say
that no player can ever be seen at his best.

George Arliss, English actor

Who is this (Alexander) Pope that I hear so much about? I cannot discover what
is his merit. Why will not my subjects write in prose! I hear a great deal too
about Shakespeare, but I cannot read him, he is such a bombast fellow.

King George II, a royal philistine if ever there was one

His violent hip-swinging during an obvious attempt to copy Elvis Presley was
revolting. Hardly the kind of performance any parent could wish their child to
witness.

The British music paper the New Musical Express *giving its*
verdict on newcomer Cliff Richard's performance on the
BBC television show Oh Boy *in 1958*

You fail to overlook the crucial point.

Samuel Goldwyn

Oh, darling. Don't . . . don't worry, darling. If . . . if you can paint, I can walk,
   anything can happen.

The line given to actress Deborah Kerr, speaking to Cary Grant
(after her character has been crippled in a road accident),
in the film An Affair To Remember *(1957)*

Maybe next year it will be Hawaiian music.

Jerry Marshall, DJ for Radio WNEW, in New York City, commenting
on the "passing" fad of rock and roll in 1955

If I were in this business only for the business, I wouldn't be in this business.

Samuel Goldwyn

That "rainbow" song is no good. It slows the picture down.

Anonymous MGM producer, after the first screening of The Wizard of Oz.

A period novel about the Civil War! Who needs the Civil War now. Who cares?

US magazine editor when offered the chance to be the first to
serialize Margaret Mitchell's novel Gone With The Wind

Calling Trevor a director is like calling Michelangelo a decorator.

Variety Club Tribute to theater director Trevor Nunn,
sent into "Pseuds' Corner" of Private Eye

Possibly some might call it a feminist novel, for the two heroines are stronger, cleverer and better-balanced than their husbands and brothers—but we are sure that Miss Cather had nothing so inartistic in mind.

> The New York Times *on* O Pioneers! *by Willa Cather, 14 September 1913*

We're going to the land of milk and honey. Anybody know the way?

> *One of the—surprisingly casual—Hebrews, about to depart from Egypt during the Exodus episode of the film* The Ten Commandments, *1956*

Written in a pseudo-criminal cant, *A Clockwork Orange* is an interesting *tour de force*, though not up to the level of the author's two previous novels.

> The New York Times *on Anthony Burgess's masterwork, 7 April 1963*

Go see that turkey for yourself, and see for yourself why you shouldn't see it.

> *Samuel Goldwyn*

Christianity will go. It will vanish and shrink. I needn't argue about that. I'm right and I'll be proved right. We're more popular than Jesus now.

> *John Lennon in March 1966, in an interview with the* London Evening Standard. *When The Beatles visited the USA, the comment was resuscitated, provoking outcry; effigies of the band were burned, and their records were banned in Bible belt states*

This makes me so sore it gets my dandruff up.

> *Samuel Goldwyn*

You're going to have a big wedding whether you like it or not. And if you don't
   like it, you don't have to come.

>   *Line spoken by the character Agnes—played by Bette Davis—*
>   *to her daughter in the film* The Catered Affair *(1956)*

The King does not get much time for reading but when he does I'm afraid he
   reads the most awful rubbish.

>   *Queen Mary to author John Buchan in 1935; only moments earlier*
>   *King George V had told Buchan, "I don't get much time for reading,*
>   *but when I do, I enjoy your books,* The Thirty-Nine Steps *and so on"*

Her works will be read with disgust by every female who has any pretensions to
   delicacy; with detestation by everyone attached to the interests of religion
   and morality, and with indignation by anyone who might feel any regard for
   the unhappy woman whose frailties should have been buried in oblivion.

>   *Anonymous, on the writer and champion of women's rights*
>   *Mary Wollstonecraft, in the* Historical Magazine, *1799*

Did you play? It sounded very good.

>   *Eugene Ormandy, conductor and music director*
>   *of the Philadelphia Orchestra*

Let's bring it up to date with some snappy nineteenth-century dialogue.

>   *Samuel Goldwyn*

Anyone who learns that bloody awful language, Welsh, well enough to make a speech, deserves our respect.

Cecil Day-Lewis, then Poet Laureate, on Prince Charles
at the time of his investiture as Prince of Wales

The scientific machinery is not very delicately constructed, and the imagination of the reader is decidedly overtaxed.

Verdict on publication of The Invisible Man *by H.G. Wells*
in The New York Times Book Review, *25 December 1897*

Yes, my wife's hands are very beautiful. I'm going to have a bust made of them.

Samuel Goldwyn

I have made love to 10,000 women.

George Simenon, author, bragger, and creator of the fictional character
Inspector Maigret (Simenon's wife said the figure was less)

Certainly no man or woman of normal mental health would be attracted by the sadistic, obscene deformations of Cézanne, Modigliani, Matisse, Gauguin and the other Fauves.

John Hemming Fry, art critic, in The Revolt Against Beauty, *1934*

I purposefully didn't do anything, and you were all behind.

Eugene Ormandy, conductor and music director
of the Philadelphia Orchestra

For the theater one needs long arms; it is better to have them too long than too short. An artiste with short arms can never, never make a fine gesture.

Sarah Bernhardt, actress

I can foresee no commercial possibilities for such a book and consequently can offer no encouragement.

Note from editor at McGraw-Hill publishers, to Dr Laurence J. Peter upon receipt of his manuscript of The Peter Principle: Why Things Always Go Wrong *(the book remained on* The New York Times *bestseller list throughout the '70s and has been translated into no fewer than 36 languages)*

We all know what it is to have a half-warmed fish inside us.

Rev. William Archibald Spooner, (he meant, "half-formed wish")

It's absolutely impossible, but it has possibilities.

Samuel Goldwyn

Louis, forget it. No Civil War picture ever made a nickel.

Irving Thalberg, MGM producer—offered film rights to Margaret Mitchell's novel Gone With The Wind—*to his boss, Louis B. Mayer*

They were a tense and peculiar family the Oedipuses, weren't they?

Max Beerbohm, English theater critic

I have nothing to say, I am saying it, and that is poetry.

John Cage, US composer of avant-garde *music, in 1972*

Of course they have, or I wouldn't be sitting here talking to someone like you.

Barbara Cartland, when asked by an interviewer whether she thought class barriers had broken down in England

I'm sorry, Mr Kipling, but you just don't know how to use the English language.

Editor of the San Francisco Examiner, *rejecting a short story by Rudyard Kipling, creator of* The Jungle Book, *among many other stories*

We have that Indian scene. We can get the Indians from the reservoir.

Samuel Goldwyn, (he meant, "reservation")

The Germans are like women, you can scarcely fathom their depths —they haven't any.

Friedrich Wilhelm Nietzsche, in The Antichrist *(1888)*

Give me a couple of years, and I'll make that actress an overnight success.

Samuel Goldwyn

It is probable that the fad (the movies) will die out in the next few years.

Comment from the American Independent, *17 March 1910*

I tell you, Elvis can't last.

Jackie Gleason in 1956

Who would want to see a play about an unhappy traveling salesman?

Cheryl Crawford, Broadway producer, when turning down Arthur Miller's play
Death of a Salesman (and rejecting Elia Kazan's offer to produce it)

No one faintly like an actress got off the train.

Studio worker sent to meet Bette Davis, who was due to arrive in Hollywood,
thinking she had failed to show

Clap your feet!

Bernie, of the pop group the Nolan Sisters

And it was this month that my book was coming out here! What attention will it get with this going on? What has happened to England? Why don't they stop the war?

Amy Lowell, poetess, lamenting the outbreak of World War I—
for all the wrong reasons

You'd better learn secretarial work or else get married.

Director of the Blue Book Modelling Agency to aspiring
young model Marilyn Monroe in 1944

Is the bean dizzy?

Rev. William Archibald Spooner, (he meant, "Is the dean busy?")

I can do anything you want me to do as long as I don't have to speak.

Linda Evangelista, supermodel

Why is everything so dirty here?

> *Samuel Goldwyn, posing a question to a film director. On being told that the set was representing a slum, Goldwyn riposted, "Well, this slum cost a lot of money"*

You never die enough to cry.

> *Jack Kerouac*

You do not need to leave your room. Remain sitting at your table and listen. Do not even listen, simply wait, be quiet, still and solitary. The world will freely offer itself to you to be unmasked, it has no choice, it will roll in ecstasy at your feet.

> *Franz Kafka*

How (not) to be Politically Correct

Sensible and responsible women do not want to vote. The relative positions to be assumed by man and woman in the working out of our civilization were assigned long ago by a higher intelligence than ours.

Grover Cleveland, former US president, 1905

From now on we shall offer police jobs to qualified women regardless of sex.

Affirmative action statement on behalf of a town in the state of New Jersey

White folks was in caves while we was building empires . . . We taught philosophy and astrology and mathematics before Socrates and them Greek homos ever got around to it.

Rev. Al Sharpton, at Kean College, New Jersey in 1994
(speech transcribed in The Forward*)*

When a lady says no, she means perhaps. When she says perhaps, she means yes. But when she says yes she is no lady.

Lord Denning, 1982

Antichrist! I renounce you and all your cults and creeds.

> *Rev. Ian Paisley interrupting Pope John Paul II in Strasbourg,*
> *while simultaneously unfurling a red banner that read*
> *"Pope John Paul II Anti-Christ"*

I ain't going to let no darkies and white folks segregate together in this town.

> *Eugene Connor, police commissioner of Birmingham, Alabama. Quoted in* The
> Observer *newspaper's "Sayings of the Week,"*
> *March 1950*

I really believe that the pagans, and the abortionists, and the feminists, and the
gays and the lesbians who are actively trying to make that an alternative
lifestyle, the ACLU, People For The American Way, all of them who have tried
to secularize America. I point the finger in their face and say, "you helped this
to happen" . . . The abortionists have got to bear some burden for this because
God will not be mocked.

> *Rev. Jerry Falwell on the Christian TV program* The 700 Club,
> *blaming a whole rash of groups for the September 11 attacks on*
> *New York and Washington. Falwell later apologized*

Nothing could be more anti-biblical than letting women vote.

> Harper's *magazine, November 1853*

Minorities, women, and the mentally-challenged are strongly advised to apply.

> *Job announcement from the US Department of the Interior,*
> *National Biological Survey*

There are only about 20 murders a year in London and not all are serious—some are just husbands killing their wives.

Commander G.H. Hatherill of Scotland Yard, February 1954

Most of these feminists are radical, frustrated lesbians, many of them, and man-haters, and failures in their relationships with men, and who have declared war on the male gender. The Biblical condemnation of feminism has to do with its radical philosophy and goals. That's the bottom line.

Jerry Falwell, US evangelist

I believe that God created man. I object to teachers saying that we came from monkeys.

Ian Paisley, April 1980

I thank heaven for a man like Adolf Hitler, who built a front line of defense against the anti-Christ of Communism.

Frank Buchman, US evangelist, August 1936

He is purple—the gay pride color, and his antenna is shaped like a triangle—the gay pride symbol.

Jerry Falwell, US evangelist, "outs" Teletubbies character Tinky Winky in the February edition of the National Liberty Journal (edited and published by Falwell. On the Today show on NBC, Falwell also told Katie Couric that to have "little boys running around with purses and acting effeminate and leaving the idea that the masculine male, the feminine female is out, and gay is OK (is something) which Christians do not agree with"

Bad weather is like rape. If it's inevitable, just relax and enjoy it.

Clayton Williams, Republican, then running for the governorship of Texas.
(Forced to account for the statement, which caused uproar, he said, "That was a
joke . . . If anyone's offended, I apologize . . . This is not a Republican woman's
club that we're having. It's a working cow camp—a tough world, where you get
kicked in the testicles if you're not careful." Eventually, he had to cave in: "I
apologize from the bottom of my heart")

If anyone understood what Hindus really believe, there would be no doubt that
they have no business administering government policies.

Pat Robertson

All homosexuals should be castrated.

Evangelist Billy Graham (Graham later apologized for this statement)

Modern women defend their office with all the fierceness of domesticity. They
fight for desk and typewriter as for the hearth and home, and develop a sort
of wolfish wifehood on behalf of the invisible head of the firm. That is why
they do office work so well; and that is why they ought not to do it.

G.K. Chesterton, from What's Wrong with the World, *1910,*
discussing a particularly threatening new "type" of woman

Feminism encourages women to leave their husbands, kill their children,
practice witchcraft, destroy capitalism and become lesbians.

Rev. Pat Robertson, speaking at the 1992 GOP Convention

Homosexual conduct is, and has been, considered abhorrent, immoral, detestable, a crime against nature, and a violation of the laws of nature and of nature's God upon which this Nation and our laws are predicated. Such conduct violates both the criminal and civil laws of this State and is destructive to a basic building block of society—the family . . . It is an inherent evil against which children must be protected.

Chief Justice Moore, Alabama Supreme Court

UFO Club, Hispanic Club . . . Native American Club, Human Rights Club . . . Young Democrats . . . UFO (Ultimate Frisbee Organization), Advancement of Hispanic Students . . . Chinese Checkers Club . . . HIS Club (Bible study club) . . . Latino Pride Club . . . Students Against Drunk Driving. . . Students of the Orient . . . Young Republicans.

Partial list of the high school clubs banned in 1996 by the Salt Lake City Board of Education in an attempt to crack down on gays and lesbians

Any nation is heathen that ain't strong enough to punch you in the jaw.

Will Rogers

Life in this society being, at best, an utter bore and no aspect of society being at all relevant to women, there remains to civic-minded, responsible, thrill-seeking females only to overthrow the government, eliminate the money system, institute complete automation, and destroy the male sex.

SCUM (Society for Cutting Up Men) manifesto—Valerie Solana

The whole thing (the Women's Suffrage Movement) is an epidemic of vanity and restlessness—a disease as marked as measles or smallpox . . . Hereafter this outbreak will stand in history as an instance of national sickness, of moral decadence, of social disorder.

Mrs Eliza Lynn Linton, US journalist, Partisans of the Wild Women,
March 1892

Heterosexual intercourse is the pure, formalized expression of contempt for women's bodies.

Andrea Dworkin

Until now it has been thought that the level of testosterone in men is normal simply because they have it. But if you consider how abnormal their behavior is, then you are led to the hypothesis that almost all men are suffering from "testosterone poisoning."

From A Feminist Dictionary*, eds. Kramarae and Treichler,*
(Pandora Press, 1985)

It is about a socialist, anti-family political movement that encourages women to leave their husbands, kill their children, practice witchcraft, destroy capitalism and become lesbians.

Pat Robertson, then presidential candidate, on the
proposed Equal Rights Amendment in Iowa

A woman is just a woman, but a good cigar is a smoke.

Rudyard Kipling

What are my assets, and what are they worth? My assets are my wife and my daughters. If I do not put a fictitious value on the goodwill of love, I have to admit that my wife is not an improving property—that is to say, she is not likely now to become more valuable to me than she has been in my home life. My daughters I must set down as a mere speculation. They may or may not turn out well.

From The Domestic Blunders of Women, *by "A Mere Man" (London, 1899)*

It might be going a little too far to say women are absolutely dishonest about money; but it is not going a bit too far to say that they have no idea how hard it is to earn, that they have no idea of its value, that they cannot save it, that they have not the remotest notion how to spend it properly, and that, therefore, they should not be entrusted with either its saving or its spending.

From The Domestic Blunders of Women, *by "A Mere Man" (London, 1899)*

Woman's participation in political life . . . would involve the domestic calamity of a deserted home and the loss of the womanly qualities for which refined men adore women and marry them . . . Doctors tell us, too, that thousands of children would be harmed or killed before birth by the injurious effect of untimely political excitement on their mothers.

Henry T. Finck, US critic, The Independent, *30 January 1901*

I've tried several varieties of sex. The conventional position makes me claustrophobic and the others give me a stiff neck or lockjaw.

Tallulah Bankhead, actress, 1972

The male chromosome is an incomplete female chromosome. In other words,
the male is a walking abortion; aborted at the gene stage. To be male is to be
deficient, emotionally limited; maleness is a deficiency disease and males are
emotional cripples.

Valerie Solanos

A woman will lie about anything, just to stay in practice.

Philip Marlowe

Women are like elephants to me: nice to look at, but I wouldn't want to own one.

W.C. Fields

You can't stay married in a situation where you are afraid to go to sleep in case
your wife might cut your throat.

Mike Tyson

My notion of a wife at 40 is that a man should be able to change her, like a
banknote, for two 20s.

Warren Beatty, 1997

Men are propelled by genetically ordained impulses over which they have no
control, to distribute their seed into as many females as possible.

Marlon Brando, 1994

How many husbands have I had? You mean apart from my own . . . ?

Zsa Zsa Gabor

The Unengaged Brain

Suddenly, I was subjected to a particularly nasty, totally unexpected and unprovoked attack.

> *Peter Sutcliffe, the Yorkshire "Ripper," in April 1983, on how he was assaulted by a fellow inmate while serving his jail sentence*

The people in the Navy look on motherhood as being compatible with being a woman.

> *Rear Admiral James R. Hogg*

One thing I can't understand is why the newspapers labelled me "The Mad Bomber." That was unkind.

> *George Matesky, on his arrest for placing 20 bombs in public places over a 17-year period, New York, Journal-American, 22 January 1957*

Will you please send someone to mend the garden path. My wife tripped and fell on it yesterday and now she is pregnant.

> *Extract from a letter to an English council's housing department*

Alan Brazil: I was sad to hear yesterday about the death of Inspector Morse, John Shaw.

TalkSport Co-Host: John Thaw, Alan.

Alan Brazil: Do you know, I've been doing that all morning. John, if you're listening, sorry mate.

Exchange on TalkSport radio

Showers (will be) bubbling up.

Gravity-defying snippet from a BBC radio weather forecast; increasingly, it has become a favourite—if slightly bizarre—phrase in such predictions

We don't necessarily discriminate. We simply exclude certain types of people.

Colonel Gerald Wellman, Reserve Officer Training Corps

God Almighty, take the vote and get it over with!

Member of the public, Richard Llamas, shouting from the Senate gallery during Clinton's impeachment trial (he was swiftly removed and arrested)

Well, you could count them on the fingers of less than one hand.

Jack Elder, New Zealand Police Minister

Many people never stop to realize that a tree is a living thing, not that different from a tall, leafy dog that has roots and is very quiet.

Jack Handey, environmentalist

Become a legally-ordained clergy person—for free online. Perform weddings, baby namings and religious services. Members in all 50 states and worldwide. Recognizing all religious traditions.

Internet plug for spiritualhumanism.org,
(the home page had a button with "Ordain Me")

I didn't intend for this to take on a political tone. I'm just here for the drugs.

Nancy Reagan, replying to an unwelcome and unrelated question at a
"Just Say No" campaign event

This is to give notice that Lord Camden does not mean to shoot himself or any of his tenants till the 14th of September.

Sign posted at Lord Camden's residence, the Hermitage, near Sevenoaks, Kent,
at the start of the sporting season of 1821, (from Blunders,
Advertisements and Epitaphs, *1880)*

I thought my window was down, but I found out it was up when I put my head through it.

Detail of the circumstances of an accident in a claim submitted
to an insurance company

Would you, my dear young friends, like to be inside with the five wise virgins, or outside, alone and in the dark with the foolish ones.

Montagu Butler, preaching to a congregation of undergraduates
at Trinity Chapel, Cambridge

(The Air Force is pleased with the performance of the C-5A cargo plane, although) having the wings fall off at eight thousand feet is a problem.

Major General Charles F. Kuyk Jr.

Had Christ died in my van, with people around him who loved him . . . (his death) would have been far more dignified.

Dr Jack Kevorkian, physician and euthanasia activist,
USA Today, *30 July 1996*

I pulled away from the side of the road, glanced at my mother-in-law and headed over the embankment.

Detail of the circumstances of an accident in a claim submitted to an insurance company

The toilet is blocked and we cannot bath the children until it is cleared.

Extract from a letter to an English council's housing department

All those magnificent balls on deck.

Retired Royal Navy officer Captain Sam Lombard-Hobson, wistfully recalling the days when smart dances were still held aboard ship, on BBC Radio 4's Today *program, June 1983. Barely stifled laughter from the presenting team followed, as presenter John Timpson, attempting a smooth transition, repeated the phrase, saying, "Ah, how well I remember those magnificent balls on deck"*

Life is indeed precious. And I believe the death penalty helps to affirm this fact.

Ed Koch, Mayor of New York City

Weight-watchers will meet at 7pm at the First Presbyterian Church. Please use the large, double door at the side entrance.

Church bulletin

Parents, you have children—or, if you have not, your daughters may have.

Impassioned temperance orator to a Boston audience
(from Bulls, Blunders and Howlers, *1928)*

If everyone on earth just stopped breathing for an hour, the greenhouse effect would no longer be a problem.

Jerry Adler, Newsweek, *31 December 1990*

And now the sequence of events, in no particular order.

Dan Rather, US anchorman, during a radio broadcast

Stephen Roche, the only British or Irish cyclist to win the Tour de France.

ITV commentator

The bride is on the right.

TV commentator, stating the obvious as Lady Diana Spencer set off
down the aisle on her father's arm on her wedding day, 1981

In Oxford, a jury has been told that Donald Neilson denied he was the Pink Panther.

BBC Radio 4 newsreader, Edward Cole, reading a headline about an alleged
murderer dubbed "The Black Panther" by the press

The reason that the World Trade Center got hit is because there are a lot of people living in abject poverty out there who don't have any hope for a better life . . . I think they (the hijackers) were brave at the very least.

Ted Turner, AOL Time Warner Vice Chairman and CNN founder, at Brown University, 11 February 2002, as reported by Gerald Carbonne in the following day's Providence Journal. *Turner then issued a statement, saying "The attacks of September 11 were despicable acts. I in no way meant to convey otherwise"*

Presenter (to palaeontologist): So what would happen if you mated the woolly mammoth with, say, an elephant?
Expert: Well in the same way that a horse and a donkey produce a mule, we'd get a sort of half-mammoth.

Exchange overhead on Greater London Radio

Will you please send a man to look at my water, it is a funny colour and not fit to drink.

Extract from a letter to an English council's housing department

Aristotle Onassis, the Greek shitting typoon.

Radio slip-up

The Chancellor of the Exchequer has just begun to announce his bunny midget.

James Alexander Gordon, BBC Radio 2 announcer, with a newsflash on the forthcoming mini-budget

More about that delay on British Rail Southern Region. We have our reporter on the line . . .

An unfortunate radio link

You are now going to hear the bum of the flightelbee.

Stuart Hibberd (attrib.), radio announcer

Presenter: So it'd be like some sort of hairy gorilla?

Expert: Er, well yes, but elephant-shaped, and with tusks.

Exchange overhead on Greater London Radio

At the present moment, the whole Fleet is lit up. When I say "lit up," I mean lit up by fairy lamps. We've forgotten the whole Royal Review. We've forgotten the Royal Review. The whole thing is lit up by fairy lamps. It's fantastic. It isn't the Fleet at all. It's just . . . it's just fairy land. The whole Fleet is in fairy land . . .

Lieutenant-Commander Tommy Woodrooffe, a leading BBC radio commentator of the 1930s, during what was to have been a 15-minute commentary of the "illumination" of the British Fleet on the night of the Coronation Naval Review at Spithead. (He was faded out after less than four minutes)

An invisible car came out of nowhere, struck my car and vanished.

Detail of an accident in a claim submitted to an insurance company

In life he was a living legend; in death, nothing has changed.

Live TV

John Snow: In a sense, Deng Xiaoping's death was inevitable, wasn't it?

Expert: Er, yes.

Channel 4 News

The weather will be cold. There are two reasons for this. One is that the
temperatures will be lower.

Radio weather forecast, 12 April 1969

And that was played by the Lindsay String Quartet . . . or at least two-thirds of
them.

Sean Rafferty, Radio 3

An end is in sight to the severe weather shortage.

Ian Macaskill, optimistic weatherman

Do you believe David Trimble will stick to his guns on decommissioning?

Interviewer, Ulster TV

Ah, the Queen has just left the bridge of HMS *Vanguard* and has gone down
below for some reason or other . . . (interminable pause) . . . and now I can see
water coming through the side of the ship . . .

*John Snagge, trying hard to spin out his commentary during the visit of the
King and Queen (George VI and Elizabeth) to Canada in 1939*

It has been the German army's largest peacetime operation since World War II.

ITN snippet

The earth is home, and all its refugees, its homeless, sometimes seem a sort of advance guard of apocalypse. They represent a principle of disintegration— the fate of homelessness generalized to a planetary scale . . . The flesh is home: African nomads without houses decorate their faces and bodies instead. The skull is home. We fly in and out of it on mental errands. The highly-developed spirit becomes a citizen of its own mobility, for home has been internalized and travels with the homeowner. Home, thus transformed: is freedom. Everywhere you lay your hat is home. Home is the bright light under the hat.

Time essay by Lance Morrow, 24 December 1990. Winner of the "Award for the Silliest Analysis" on the Media Research Center's "Notable Quotables" website

Israeli troops have this morning entered the Arab township of Hebron, in search of the perpetrators of the recent suicide bomb attacks.

Snippet from CNN News

Goods are shitting on the supermarket shelves.

Sue Lloyd-Roberts, ITN

Ladies and gentlemen: the President of the United States—Hoobert Herver!

American radio announcer Harry von Zell, welcoming President Herbert Hoover at the microphone

This afternoon there will be a meeting in the south and north ends of the church. Children will be baptized at both ends.

Church bulletin

I was on my way to the doctor with rear end trouble when my universal joint
gave way causing me to have an accident.

> Detail of the "accident in question" in a claim submitted
> to an insurance company

Has anyone here been raped and speaks English?

> Crass TV reporter in the Congo in 1960, among a crowd of Belgian
> civilians during the war of independence. The phrase became the
> title of a book by Edward Behr in 1978

In New Hampshire, closest Senate race in the country, this race between Dick
Swett and Bob Smith is hot and tight as a too-small bathing suit on a too-long
car ride back from the beach.

> Dan Rather, during CBS News election night coverage, 5 November 1996

There she is, the huge vast bulk of her.

> Wynford Vaughan-Thomas of the BBC, as—unfortunately—the camera
> moved to a close-up of the late HRH the Queen Mother during the
> launching of the Ark Royal

Is your SUV a weapon of terrorism? Some people think so. They're taking out
ads to tell you why . . . coming up in our next half-hour, is your SUV a weapon
of mass destruction?

> Lester Holt, fill-in co-host, plugging a segment on how buying
> Middle East oil aids terrorism on US Today program

Well, am I a liberal, a conservative, or what? What . . . I believe in sunny summer mornings when the grass is sweet and the wind is green with possibilities. I believe in chili with no beans and iced tea all year round . . . I believe music is too important to be left to musicians, and that Ella Fitzgerald is the best American singer ever, and that Beethoven would have liked Chuck Berry . . . And so it goes.

Linda Ellerbee in her first commentary on CNN, 20 March 1989

"These boat people," says the government of Hong Kong. "They all want to go to America." Well, I swear I don't know why, do you? I mean take Vietnam. Why would any Vietnamese come to America after what America did for Vietnam? Don't they remember My Lai, napalm, Sylvester Stallone? Clearly they have no more sense over there than, say, Mexicans who keep trying to get into this country even though this country stole large parts of their country in the first place.

"Analysis" by Linda Ellerbee, CNN PrimeNews, *2 June 1989*

President Carter has painful haemorrhoids and is being treated by his physician, Rear Admiral, er . . . William Lookass . . . Lukash . . . ?

US newscaster

I am a single woman living in a downstairs flat and would be pleased if you could do something about the noise made by the man I have on top of me every night.

Extract from a letter to an English council's housing department

The other car collided with mine without giving warning of its intentions.

Detail of the "accident in question" in an insurance claim

Please send a man with clean tools to finish the job and satisfy the wife.

Extract from a letter to an English council's housing department

Thousands may have been gunned down in Beijing, but what about the millions of American kids whose lives are being ruined by an enormous failure of the country's educational system . . . We can and we should agonize about the dead students in Beijing, but we've got a much bigger problem here at home.

John Chancellor's commentary on NBC Nightly News, 20 June 1989

Rolls-Royce announced today that it is recalling all Rolls-Royce cars made after 1966 because of faulty nuts behind the steering wheels.

Walter Cronkite, famously gaffe-prone US anchorman

Susan, things are washing up on the shore that have never seen the light of day in a long time.

From a local news report on the after-effects of Hurricane Hugo in 1989

And so it was woo-woo and goodbye train.

Dan Rather, wrapping up CBS Evening News, 16 May 2001,
with an item on a runaway freight train

Today Lesbian forces invaded . . . no, sorry, that should be Lesbianese.

From a British news report on the conflict in the Lebanon

The flights, landings and take-off of airships called "flying saucers" and "flying cigars" of any nationality are forbidden on the territory of the community of Châteauneuf-du-Pape.

Decree by the Mayor of Châteauneuf-du-Pape, France 31 October, 1954

A squid, as you know, of course, has ten testicles.

Graham Kerr, Canadian TV chef on the cookery programme
The Galloping Gourmet

We are going to play a hiding and finding game. Now, are your balls high up or low down? Close your eyes a minute and dance around, and look for them. Are they high up? Or are they low down? If you have found your balls, toss them over your shoulder and play with them.

BBC children's radio Music and Movement *program in the 1950s*

She was practicing fastest finger first by herself in bed last night.

Chris Tarrant, describing UK Who Wants To Be A Millionaire *winner Judith Keppel, on* This Morning

That should a member be unable to write, he might authorize another person to frank for him, provided that on the back of the letter so franked, the member gives a certificate, under his hand, of his inability to write.

A Bill introduced in 1784, sent from the Parliament of Ireland for royal approbation (from Bulls, Blunders and Howlers, *1928)*

Those disgraceful Madonna pictures—four-page special inside.

The Sun newspaper

So, you're in drapes?

American tourist to John Burton, Surveyor of the Fabric
of Westminster Abbey

My mom tells me we're descended from Edward the Confessor.

Young American student to this author, during her days as tour manager, while
visiting the Tower of London. Edward "the Confessor" died without issue

He wouldn't like that; my husband was a very private person.

Widow to Bishop's Chaplain on being told that her local church's cemetery was
full, leaving the public cemetery as the other burial option

The space in the graveyard being now limited, no-one will be buried in future
except those that live in the parish.

From Bulls, Blunders and Howlers, 1928

Too many bugs and leeches and spiders and spider webs. Please spray the
wilderness to rid the area of these pests.

Comment on a feedback form from the US Forest Service

I have had the Clerk of the Works down on the floor six times, but still have no
satisfaction.

Extract from a letter to an English council's housing department

I didn't know petrol was highly inflammable.

> *Taxi driver Saqib Bashir, who bought 80 liters of petrol during a fuel shortage in late 2000. Bashir then stored it in plastic containers in an empty house owned by him. The fuel melted the plastic, leaked and fire fighters—alerted by neighbors who could smell fumes—fearing an explosion, evacuated the street in Derby, England. The clean-up operation cost over £100,000. Bashir pleaded guilty at Derby Magistrates court to four charges of unlawful storage of fuel and one charge under Health and Safety laws. Reported in the* Darwin Awards

Pumping is the devil's pastime, and we must all say no to Satan. Inflate your tires by all means, but then hide your bicycle pump where it cannot tempt you.

> *Spokesman for the Nakhon Ratchasima hospital in Thailand, reported in the* Japan Times, *16 April 1997*

The Queen is not a fairy.

> *Buckingham Palace spokesman, explaining the large numbers of vaccinations and pills prescribed to the Queen*

My great-grandfather was baptized in the Church of England, married in the Church of England and buried in a Church of England graveyard.
And so was I.

> *Prospective MP for Walthamstow, south London, in the early 1900s, at pains to stress his religious affiliation (from* Bulls, Blunders and Howlers, *1928)*

The telephone pole was approaching. I was attempting to swerve out of its way when it struck the front end.

Detail of the "accident in question" in a claim submitted
to an insurance company

A McDonald's would be nice at the trailhead.

Comment on a feedback form from the US Forest Service

Presenter: Name a red liquid.

Contestant: Mercury.

Presenter: Is Mercury red? Let's see if it's there . . . no, bad luck. I didn't think it was red.

Contestant: I wasn't sure if it was red or green.

Exhange on ITV programme Family Fortunes—
reported in the "Dumb Britain" section of Private Eye

Dear and Fair Madam,

I have much pleasure to inform you that my dearly unfortunate wife will no longer be under your kind treatment. She having left this world for the other on the night of the 27th.

For your help in this matter I shall remain grateful.

Yours reverently...

Letter received by the superintendent of a hospital for sick women in India.
(Babujee Writes Home, *1935*)

I was sued by a woman who claimed that she became pregnant because she watched me on television and I bent her contraceptive coil.

Uri Geller

I wish to report that tiles are missing from the roof of the outside toilet and I think it was bad wind the other night that blew them off.

Extract from a letter to an English council's housing department

The ladies of the church have cast off clothing of every kind. They can be seen in the church basement this Saturday.

Church bulletin

What time do the penguins leave the zoo?

Question asked in a tourist information centre in Scotland

Does the river follow the canyon the whole way down?

Question asked of a river guide accompanying a group rafting down the Colorado River in the American Grand Canyon

Listener: My most embarrassing moment was when my artificial leg fell off at the altar on my wedding day.
Simon Fanshawe: How awful! Do you still have an artificial leg?

Exchange on the UK's Talk Radio station

A respectable young woman wants washing.

Small ad in a nineteenth-century English provincial newspaper

A cat charity (in North London) says fewer people are taking in homeless cats—
and they're blaming it on the war in Iraq and congestion charging.

> Wood Green Weekly Herald. *Entry sent into "Warballs" column of* Private Eye

The Queen is a hot potato.

> *The Archbishop of Canterbury, on why the subject of the Queen*
> *should be treated with the utmost discretion*

You guys are working on the Fourth of July? I can't believe it! Don't you
celebrate it?

> *Question asked of an English employee by an American*
> *employee of an international company*

We have a copy of the list of 1,800 names, and any ex-serviceman wishing to see
if his name is in the list can call into the shop under the office and see it.

> *Notice in the* Western News and Galway Leader, *during World War I,*
> *giving news that the* Leader *had a full list of the men of the*
> *Connaught Rangers who had lost their lives*

Beware! To touch these wires is instant death. Anyone found doing so will be
prosecuted.

> *Sign at a US railroad station*

The guy was all over the road. I had to swerve a number of times before I hit
him.

> *Detail of the "accident in question" in an insurance claim*

Interviewer: So did you see which train crashed into which train first?

Fifteen-year-old: No, they both ran into each other at the same time.

Snippet from BBC Radio 4

If in the future your circumstances alter, please contact this office.

Extract from a letter sent by Bolton Council, Lancashire, to pensioner
Edith Platt, rejecting her application for a house improvement grant—
because she was dead

We are getting married in September and would like it in the garden before we move into the house.

Extract from a letter to an English council's housing department

Your food stamps will be stopped effective March 1992 because we received notice that you passed away. May God bless you. You may re-apply if there is a change in your circumstances.

Letter from the Department of Social Services, Greenville, South Carolina

(Hereby decreed illegal all): public flatulence, crepitation, gaseous emission, and miasmic effluence.

Alaskan legislature outlawing the act of "flatulating"
in public (or breaking wind)

I am very annoyed that you have branded my son illiterate. This is a dirty lie, as I was married a week before he was born.

Letter to California Department of Human Resource Development

The most surprising thing about the rehearsal is how Macy (Gray) keeps it together—ringmaster, not freakshow. She is so good at it that she lies down on one of the sofas and simultaneously sings, gives directions and reads a novel. She is both very present and in her own world. Watching her read her book and keep the beat, I realize that it is possible to coexist with humanity and be totally mentally divergent.

Emma Forest, reporting in the Telegraph Magazine—
sent into "Pseuds' Corner" section of Private Eye

Latest Telegraphic News—Fifty French prefects have been hanged.
Newspaper headline in a West Indian paper in the 1880s, based on a telegram wired in from a French source (the prefects had, in fact, been suspended— suspendus *and not hanged—*pendus*)*

Wanted: A Sorrel Colt, suitable for Young Lady with a long tail.
From the "Wanted" page of a nineteenth-century English provincial newspaper

Wanted: A Man and his Wife to look after a Farm, and a Dairy with a religious turn of mind without incumbrance.
From the "Wanted" page of a nineteenth-century English provincial newspaper

Can you copy the Internet onto this disk for me?
Customer in a computer shop

A miller writes: Two weeks ago I was full of rats, and now I haven't one.

Testimonial placed in a newspaper by a nineteenth-century manufacturer
of vermin powder in order to advertise the proprietor's good services

Coming home I drove into the wrong house and collided with a tree I don't have.

Detail of the "accident in question" in a claim submitted
to an insurance company

He called attention to the number of ownerless dogs about the streets, and
urged that the police should have instructions to destroy them, or order dogs,
with owners, to be muzzled.

From the Birmingham Daily Post, *in the nineteenth century*

During the celebration a child was run over, wearing a short red dress, which
never spoke afterwards.

Notice in a nineteenth-century newspaper

You be *libertas*, I be *patria*.

How the Washington Post *reported the famous Latin phrase Ubi libertas,*
ibi patria, pronounced by a certain Mr Curtis as he unveiled the Sedgewick
Monument at West Point

Mr. Gibson carefully locked up his horse, which is a wooden and iron building.

Passage from the Natal Mercury, *12 November 1883*

The captain swum ashore from the vessel and subsequently saved the life of the stewardess; she was insured for fifteen thousand dollars and was full of railroad iron.

Notice in a nineteenth-century newspaper

We were going to put "God Bless the Prince of Wales" right through our Welsh humbug rock, but we decided it wouldn't be appropriate.

Shopkeeper in Caernarfon, Wales, the town where the investiture of Prince Charles as Prince of Wales took place

Wanted, a furnished room for a single gentleman looking both ways and well ventilated.

Advertisement recorded in Bulls, Blunders and Howlers, *1928*

He was of accidental character, and the jury returned a verdict of excellent death.

*English country newspaper in the nineteenth century
(the words in italics were, of course, transposed)*

Whasssup!

*Trooper Luke Pagan, Horse Guard of the Queen's Blues and Royals,
reaching the end of his tether and bellowing the Budweiser beer slogan in
Whitehall, central London, after being pestered by a British
TV film crew. Following his outburst, he was carpeted by his Commanding
Officer for breaking army rules of silence*

So the congregation resolved upon a European trip for their beloved pastor, and on Saturday night made him acquainted with the delightful fact. Accompanying the report of the Committee was a nicely-filled purse, which was placed at the disposal of the pastor, who, after thanking them, made a turn down South Main Street as far as Planet, then up Planet to Benefit Street, where he was caught by some boys, who tied a tin pan to his tail. Away he went again, up Benefit Street, and down College, at the foot of which he was shot by a policeman.

> *The* American Providence Daily Journal *in the 1850s, muddling up the type set for two very different stories—one, about a departing clergyman; the other, about a mad dog let loose on the streets*

This is to let you know that our lavatory seat is broken and we can't get BBC2.

> *Extract from a letter to an English council's housing department*

Remember in prayer the many who are sick of our church and community.

> *Slip-up in the delivery of the usual notices during a church service*

The choir invites any member of the congregation who enjoys sinning to join the choir.

> *Church bulletin, with an unfortunate misprint*

I collided with a stationary truck coming the other way.

> *Detail of the "accident in question" in an insurance claim*

The Roman Catholics claim to be making material advances in Africa, particularly in Algeria, where they have as many as 185,000 adherents and a Missionary Society for Central Africa. During the past three years they have obtained a firm footing in the interior of the continent, and have sent forth several missionaries into the equatorial regions. They are accustomed to begin their work by buying heathen children and educating them. The easiest and best way to prepare them is to first wipe them with a clean towel; then place them in dripping pans and bake them until they are tender. Then you will have no difficulty in rubbing them through a sieve, and will save them by not being obliged to cut them into slices and cook for several hours.

A typesetting gaffe in a Montreal paper in the nineteenth century, when the setter mixed up an article on Catholic advances in Africa with a recipe for making tomato catsup

The associate minister unveiled the church's new tithing campaign slogan last Sunday: "I Upped My Pledge—Up yours."

Church bulletin

The pedestrian had no idea which way to run, so I ran over him.

Detail of the "accident in question" in a claim submitted to an insurance company

Business—
and how to get behind in it

We don't pay taxes. Only the little people pay taxes.

> *Leona Helmsley (dubbed "the Queen of Mean,") widow and heir of the*
> *New York real estate tycoon, Henry Helmsley, and one of the richest women in*
> *the United States. This fact notwithstanding, Helmsley was convicted of*
> *mail fraud and tax evasion in the 1990s and was sentenced to*
> *18 months' imprisonment (furthermore, in 2002 she was sued for $11.7 million*
> *by a former employee)*

Dear Rich Bastard . . .

> *Employee's choice of "example addressee" field when setting up*
> *a template for letters destined for wealthy clients of . . . a large bank*

Had cancer, been a pain, now pregnant.

> *Management meeting at Schroder Salomon Smith Barney summing up the*
> *career of employee Julie Bower in June 2002—who then sued them*
> *and won £1.4m*

In all likelihood, world inflation is over.

> *Dr. Per Jacobsson, Managing Director of the IMF*
> *(International Monetary Fund), in October 1959*

This company is not bust. We are merely in a cyclical decline.

> *Lord Stokes, then Chairman of ailing firm British Leyland.*
> The Observer *newspaper, "Quotes of the Year," 1974*

Now that's a nice compliment from a lass, isn't it?

> *Bradley Chait's comment added to a sexually explicit e-mail exchange between*
> *him and his (then) girlfriend, Claire Swire (both employees at an international*
> *law firm), December 2000. Chait forwarded the message to friends, and on—and*
> *on—it went across the Internet; eventually, Swire's graphically worded e-mail*
> *confession had been read by an estimated one million people*

Murdoch is a monster.

> *Charles Douglas-Home, describing Ruper Murdoch before accepting*
> *the editorship of* The Times *newspaper under . . .*
> *the very same media tycoon*

I sometimes wonder whether the British traveler does really need a seat.

> *E.C. Cox, of the British Southern Railway Co., 1926*

I'll tell you, it's Big Business. If there is one word to describe Atlantic City, it's
Big Business. Or two words—Big Business.

> *Donald Trump, American real estate tycoon*

Caution: blade is extremely sharp. Keep out of children.

> *Warning on knife blade manufactured by Olfa Corporation—the notice won the*
> *Dunce Award from SPELL (US Society for the Preservation of English*
> *Language and Literature)*

FOR SALE: Three donkeys, to be seen at a Pen, near Kingston.

TURNBULL, LEE, AND MUDON

> *Advertisement containing an unfortunate coincidence of numbers—placed by a*
> *respected firm of auctioneers, which happened to be made up of a trio of*
> *partners. Appeared in the* Jamaica Budget *of 16 June 1879*

As far as we know, our computer has never had an undetected error.

> *Weisert*

You furnish the pictures and I'll furnish the war.

> *William Randolph Hearst, issuing instructions to Frederic Remington*
> *in Cuba prior to the sinking of USS Maine, March 1898*

But what . . . is it good for?

> *Robert Lloyd, engineer at the Advanced Computing Systems Division*
> *of IBM, 1968, commenting on the microchip*

Nor are computers going to get much faster.

> *Dr Arthur L. Samuel, "The Banishment of Paper Work,"*
> New Scientist, *1964*

This paper will propose that the brand is a complex object that functions as the interface of a complex, non-linear system of production. It will argue that the brand comprises the diagram of a dynamic system of relations between products: a mechanism for exploiting the differentiation in time of a process of production through techniques of product qualification and re-qualification. The implications of considering the brand as an interface for the communication of information between producers and consumers will also be considered.

Brunel University seminar—entry sent into "Pseuds' Corner" of Private Eye

The question of whether computers can think is like the question of whether submarines can swim.

Edsgar Dijkstra

Kidneys of the chef.

Appetising item on the menu of the Cathedral Restaurant in Granada, Spain

I think that's a bit too many. I don't think there are 49 Finns that can sing.

Alain Levy, Chief Executive of EMI Records, after the ailing company,
which had shed 1,800 jobs, discovered how many artists it
had under contract in Finland

The worst crime against working people is a company that fails to operate at a profit.

Samuel Gompers—forgetting that it all depends on where the profits go

In life, there are all colors and the Teletubbies are a reflection of that . . . There are no nationalities in the Teletubbies—they are techno-babies, but they are supposed to reflect life in that sense.

> *Nick Underwood, of* Teletubbies *Marketing, to the* Daily Express. *The quote won him a "Foot in Mouth Award" from the British Plain English Campaign*

Mushrooms cultivated on substrate from extensive agriculture which is permitted in organic farming during a transitional period.

> *A label on a packet of mushrooms sold in upmarket supermarket chain Waitrose*

Efforts to assign a primary causal role to tobacco use on the basis of statistical associations ignore all the unknowns and focus undue attention on tobacco use.

> *Clarence Cook Little, Director of the Tobacco Industry Research Committee, in 1958*

With over fifty foreign cars already on sale here, the Japanese auto industry isn't likely to carve out a big slice of the US market.

> *Prediction by* Business Week, *August 1968*

I don't know that I'm in the twentieth century—I may be in the eighteenth or twenty-first.

> *Ian Macgregor, Chairman of British Steel, January 1981*

Question: Do you support the overthrow of the government by force, subversion, or violence?

Respondent: Violence.

Allegedly genuine entry, on a prospective employee's job application form

We've got to pause and ask ourselves: How much clean air do we need?

Lee Iacocca, chairman of the Chrysler Corporation

And the next train arriving on platform four is the Dunblane train. This train is very overcrowded, so if there are any passengers standing in the doorways, just throw them out the way.

Tannoy announcement at Haymarket station, Edinburgh

The point is that you can't be too greedy.

Donald Trump

It needs to be said that the poor are poor because they don't have enough money.

Sir Keith Joseph, one of Margaret Thatcher's trusted advisors speaking in March 1970

I predict the Internet will soon go spectacularly supernova and in 1996 catastrophically collapse.

Bob Metcalfe, InfoWorld, 1995

This is a message for all passengers in the fourth carriage: can you please teach
the gentleman who keeps trying to open the doors exactly how they close,
preferably by holding him firmly and letting them close repeatedly on his
head.

Announcement by driver of a London Underground train

I'm a bit of a Barnum. I make stars out of everyone.

Donald Trump, real estate tycoon, on his former lovers

They don't suffer. They can't even speak English.

*George F. Baer, railroad industrialist, answering a reporter's question
about the plight of starving miners*

People can have (the Model T in) any colour . . . so long as it's black.

*Henry Ford, founder of the Ford Motor Company. The company was forced to
move with the times, introducing a choice of colors in 1925. Though from 1909
the range had a singular look to it*

History is more or less bunk. It's tradition.

Henry Ford, in an interview with Charles N. Wheeler in 1916

We're going to try to get the boys out of the trenches by Christmas. I've
chartered a ship, and some of us are going to Europe.

*Henry Ford in 1915—a comment which resulted in the newspaper headline,
"Great War Ends Christmas Day. Ford To Stop It"*

We will never make a 32-bit operating system.

Bill Gates, Microsoft CEO, at the launch of MSX

No forbearance of failure by the Employer at any time to require performance of any provision of the Agreement or to enforce strictly the obligations of the Employee or to take action to suspend the Employee or to determine the Agreement forthwith upon discovering cause therefore shall effect the right of the Employer so to do any time and no waiver by the Employer of any condition or breach of any clause whether by conduct or otherwise shall constitute a continuing or further waiver of any such condition or breach or as the breach of any other clause.

Clause in a proposed employment contract within the Gleeds Group, management consultants. As reported by the British Plain English Campaign

E-mail is not to be used to pass on information or data. It should only be used for company business.

Memo from the accounting manager, Electric Boat Company

No Va.

The reason the Chevrolet Nova, manufactured by General Motors, was selling so slowly in Spanish-speaking territories was because the ad was telling consumers, it "Won't Go" (No Va). Vauxhall subsequently fell into the same trap with its hatchback of the same name

What I need is a list of specific, unknown problems we will encounter.

Memo from Lykes Lines Shipping

As of tomorrow, employees will only be able to access the building using
individual security cards. Pictures will be taken next Wednesday and
employees will receive their cards in two weeks.

Sun Microsystems memo

No one really understands what's going on with all these numbers.

*David Stockman, business whiz kid and Reagan advisor, in a foolishly frank
interview given to a reporter from the US magazine* Atlantic Monthly *in 1981.
It was one of many unguarded gaffes (most famously, "Reaganomics aren't
working") made by him*

Doing it right is no excuse for not meeting the schedule. No one will believe you
solved this problem in one day! We've been working on it for months. Now, go
act busy for a few weeks and I'll let you know when it's time to tell them.

R&D supervisor, 3M Corporation

I've got smoke coming from the back of my terminal. Do you guys have a fire
downtown?

Call to IT support manager within a large bank

How Anyone Can Stop Paying Income Taxes.

*Title of 1983 American bestseller by Irwin Schiff (the IRS shortly
afterwards issued him with a bill for $200,000)*

I think there is a world market for maybe five computers.

Thomas Watson, chairman of IBM (International Business Machines), 1943

Pepsi brings your ancestors back from the grave.

> *Foolish translation for the Chinese version of a US poster campaign for Pepsi,*
> *which in America had read, "Come Alive with Pepsi." (In Germany, the slogan*
> *was only marginally better: "Come alive out of the grave with Pepsi")*

Compare our prices before purchasing elsewhere.

> *Sign on shop in Jermyn Street, Piccadilly (recorded in* Bulls,
> Blunders and Howlers, *1928)*

The cup holder in my PC is broken and I am within my warranty period. How do
I go about getting that fixed?

> *Caller contacting technical support at Novell NetWire SysOp. The caller was, of*
> *course, referring to the load drawer of the machine's CD-Rom drive*

You get more out of life with a Kensitas.

> *Advertising slogan of that cigarette brand in the 1950s*

The reason Japanese people are so short and have yellow skins is because they
have eaten nothing but fish and rice for two thousand years . . . if we eat
McDonald's hamburgers and potatoes for a thousand years we will become
taller, our skin become white and our hair blonde.

> *Den Fujita, president of McDonald's in Japan, during the "McLibel" trial*

Optional modem required.

> *Notice on a computer software package*

So we went to Atari and said, "Hey, we've got this amazing thing, even built with some of your parts, and what do you think about funding us? Or we'll give it to you. We just want to do it. Pay our salary, we'll come work for you." And they said, "No." So then we went to Hewlett-Packard, and they said, "Hey, we don't need you. You haven't got through college yet."

> *Steve Jobs, Apple Computer Inc. co-founder, on attempts to get Atari and Hewlett-Packard to take an interest in his and Steve Wozniak's personal computer*

Get your feet off my desk, get out of here, you stink, and we're not going to buy your product.

> *Joe Keenan, president of Atari, to Steve Jobs, 1976*

Stocks have reached what looks like a permanently high plateau.

> *Irving Fisher, Professor of Economics, Yale University, speaking on 17 October 1929—the Wall Street Crash occurred on the 29 October 1929*

Cod Pieces.

> *Suggested name put forward in a sales campaign for new fish products being marketed by the frozen food company Birds Eye, in 1976*

McDonald's food is nutritious (and) healthy . . . (It) provides nutrients and can be a part of a healthy, balanced diet.

> *David Green, Senior Vice-President of Marketing, USA, for McDonalds, during the 'Mclibel' trial. He admitted that Coca-Cola could also be healthy, "provide nutrients" and be "part of a healthy, balanced diet"*

A receptacle having at least one exterior surface and a plurality of walls defining a discrete object receiving volume.

> *An (unnamed) lawyer's suggested phrasing, in a patent application, with which to replace the word "container."As reported by the British Plain English Campaign*

I can see (the dumping of waste) to be a benefit, otherwise you will end up with lots of vast, empty gravel pits all over the country.

> *Ed Oakley, Chief Purchasing Officer for McDonald's UK, on the company's supposedly green recycling policy, during the "McLibel" trial*

Hens kept in batteries are better cared for . . .

> *Ed Oakley on McDonald's UK's policy of buying eggs from battery-farmed hens*

I think that the free enterprise system is absolutely too important to be left to the voluntary action of the market place.

> *Richard Kelly, US Congressman*

Unfortunately for you lot, we are now stuck behind a broken-down train. We'll be here for quite a while. But I don't care: I'm now on overtime.

> *Announcement by driver of a London Underground train*

A man who has a million dollars is as well off as if he were rich.

> *John Jacob Astor (attrib.) US property tycoon and one of the most famous casualties of the* Titanic

A short lease means a lease which is not a long lease.

Blindingly obvious phrase in Income Tax Act, 1952

This was a very large corporation. It would be impossible to know everything going on.

Jeffrey K Skilling, formerly chief executive of the now-disgraced Enron

There is no reason anyone would want a computer in their home.

Ken Olson, president, chairman and founder of Digital Equipment Corporation,
at the Convention of the World Future Society in Boston in 1977

You want to have consistent and uniform muscle development across all of your muscles? It can't be done. It's just a fact of life. You just have to accept inconsistent muscle development as an unalterable condition of weight training.

Response to Arthur Jones, who solved the "insurmountable" problem
by inventing the Nautilus system

Gros Jos.

Proposed French–Canadian brand name for the "Big John's" canned pork and
beans made by Hunt Wesson Foods. Unfortunately, it translated colloquially
into "Big Tits"

Do not look into laser with remaining eye.

Warning notice on a laser-pointer device

This project is important; we can't let things that are more important interfere with it.

> *Useful suggestion on how to learn to prioritize by*
> *advertising manager, United Parcel Service*

I can confirm that you have not informed us a conservatory that has never been built and that you have not been charged any extra for one built.

> *Extract from a letter from Halifax General Insurance Services Ltd,*
> *as reported by the British Plain English Campaign*

Beginners will find that the computer is logical to a disagreeable and intensely frustrating degree.

> *Student Notes for OSIRIS II*

BRANIFF MEANS BUSINESS.

> *Advertisement that appeared in* The Times *newspaper on 13 May 1982 —*
> *unfortunately, the day after the airline had gone bust*

The cognitive measurement of consumer criteria for manufacturer parameter values in biscuit texture.

> *Impenetrable title of a research paper investigating whether*
> *crunchy biscuits taste better than soft ones*

Teamwork is a lot of people doing what "I" say.

> *Marketing executive, Citrix Corporation, demonstrating*
> *how to be a team player*

If there are any points on which you require explanation or further particulars we shall be glad to furnish such additional details as may be required by telephone.

In other words, "ring us if you have any further queries"

A cookie store is a bad idea. Besides, the market research reports say America likes crispy cookies, not soft and chewy cookies like you make.

Response to Debbi Fields' idea of launching Mrs. Fields'
Cookies as a business venture

Following a nuclear attack on the United States, the United States Postal Service plans to distribute Emergency Change of Address Cards.

US Federal Emergency Management Agency Executive Order (No. 11490)

For the purpose of this Part of this Schedule a person over pensionable age, not being an insured person, shall be treated as an employed person if he would be an insured person were he under pensionable age and would be an employed person were he an insured person.

National Insurance Act, 1964—Schedule 1, Part II

The benefit of having dedicated subject matter experts who are able to evangelize the attributes and business imperatives of their products is starting to bear fruit.

Announcement related to company restructuring by Marconi's EMEA (Europe,
Middle East, Africa and Australasia) division

(You agree) that we shall not be discharged or released from our obligations under this deed by any arrangement or agreement made between you and the contractor or a receiver, administrative receiver, administrator, liquidator or similar officer of the contractor, or by any re-negotiation, substitution, alteration, amendment or variation (however fundamental) and whether or not to our disadvantage, to or of, the obligations imposed upon the contractor or any other person or by any forbearance granted to you by the contractor or any other person as to payment, time, performance or otherwise by any release or variation (however fundamental) of, any invalidity in, or any failure to take, perfect or enforce any other indemnity, guarantee or security in respect of the obligations to which this deed relates or by any other matter or thing which but for this provision might exonerate us and this notwithstanding that such arrangement, agreement, renegotiation, substitution, alteration, amendment, variation, forbearance, matter or thing may have been made, granted or happened without our knowledge or assent.

A single clause from a deed of indemnity (the remainder withheld to preserve sanity)

There are people who don't like capitalism, and people who don't like PCs. But there's no one who likes the PC who doesn't like Microsoft.

Bill Gates

Lucent is endeavorily [sic] determined to promote constant attention on current procedures of transacting business focusing emphasis on innovative ways to better, if not supersede, the expectations of quality.

Statement from Lucent Technologies

It is a project which, as far as I can see, has a viable marketing opportunity
ahead of it.

> *Giles Shaw, Northern Ireland Minister of Commerce, speaking in 1979 about the*
> *De Lorean—the motor car nobody wanted to buy (except the makers of the* Back
> To The Future *films)*

A billion here, a billion there—sooner or later it adds up to real money.

> *Everett Dirksen*

The wines at our hotel shall leave you nothing to hope for.

> *Promising notice in a continental hotel*

Lunch and Learn Seminar: "Who's controlling your life?" (Get your manager's
permission before attending.)

> *Flyer promoting attendance at a corporate seminar*

They're multi-purpose. Not only do they put the clips on, but they take them off.

> *Explanation from Pratt & Whitney on why they charged the*
> *US Air Force nearly $1,000 for a pair of pliers*

WE LOVE YOU VERY MUCH + MOM IS DEAD.

> *Telegram conveying "birthday greetings" sent by Western Union in 1983.*
> *It should have read WE LOVE YOU VERY MUCH + MOM AND DAD;*
> *it didn't, and the company was sued for the emotional trauma caused*

We hung in on napalm when it didn't mean anything to us business-wise. The government asked us to make it and we did. We believed in the principle.

President of Dow Chemical Co., kicking back at what he saw as persistent and unjustifiable attacks on the chemical industry

That mail that used to be handled by hand, now it's handled manually.

John Hinnes, chief executive of An Post

This product is not to be used in bathrooms.

Warning notice on a bathroom heater manufactured by Holmes Co.

We know that communication is a problem. But the company is not going to discuss it with the employees.

Switching supervisor, AT&T Long Lines Division

What we are doing is in the interest of everybody, bar possibly the consumer.

Aer Lingus spokesperson

Do not dangle the mouse by its cable or throw the mouse at co-workers.

Handy instruction in a user's manual for an SGI computer

640K ought to be enough for anybody.

Attributed to Bill Gates, Microsoft CEO, in 1981, but believed to be an urban legend

The next train arriving on platform two is the Virgin train to (destination),
driven by Widow Twanky.

Tannoy announcement at Haymarket station, Edinburgh

Ladies given fits upstairs.

Notice in a Chinese tailor's shop window (from Babujee Writes Home, *1935)*

Don't Kill Your Wife with Work.
Let Electricity Do it!

London Electricity poster

Nothing sucks like an Electrolux!

*Electrolux's first marketing campaign for the firm's vacuum cleaners in the US.
The Swedish-speaking team who came up with the slogan didn't realize that
"sucks" is not the greatest virtue in the States*

Caution: Cape does not enable user to fly.

Warning notice on the Batman costume made by Kenner Products

This is the end of Western civilization.

*Lewis Douglas, US budget director, on learning that Franklin D. Roosevelt was
intending to take the United States off the gold standard in 1933*

Advertising board No. 1: VD is deadly.
Advertising board No. 2: I got it at the Co-Op.

An unfortunate juxtaposition of billboard advertising posters

For sale: Surgical instruments. Complete assortment of lately deceased
surgeons.

Small ad.

Gentlemen's throats cut with very sharp razors, with great care and skill.
No irritating feelings afterwards.
A trial solicited.

Notice in an Indian barber's shop window (from Babujee Writes Home, *1935)*

Mr R., furrier, begs to announce that he will make up capes, gowns, etc., for
ladies out of their own skins.

Advertisement recorded in Bulls, Blunders and Howlers, *1928*

Could we have a crash *à la* 1929? The flat answer is "no."

Dr Pierre A. Rinfret, economics expert, quoted in Time *magazine, 5 October
1987—"Black Monday" followed shortly after, on 19 October*

When the baby is done drinking it must be unscrewed and laid in a cool place
under a tap. If the baby does not thrive on fresh milk, it must be boiled.

Advertisement of a baby's feeding bottle (reported in Bulls,
Blunders and Howlers, *1928)*

And, you know, I just—I love real estate. It's tangible, it's solid, it's beautiful. It's
artistic, from my standpoint, and I just love real estate.

*Donald Trump, real estate tycoon, in an interview with co-host
Geoff Colvin of* Wall $treet Week *with* Fortune, *July 2002*

This is your captain speaking. Is there anyone aboard who can lend me fifty quid?

> *Unnamed pilot of a chartered British holiday jet on its way to Malaga, in Spain, which was forced to make an emergency landing in Morocco after running low on fuel (after abortive attempts to land at Seville, in Spain, and Faro, in Portugal). He had used his own travelers' cheques to pay for the fuel and now, still finding himself £50 short, was obliged to ask for a whip-round from the 166 passengers on board his aircraft (this, after the authorities refused to accept his credit card for the £600 fuel bill)*

Golden ripe, boneless bananas, 39 cents a pound.

> *Advertisement*

I am sorry for the delay to this service. This is due to signal problems. And if you look out to the right-hand side of the train, you will see the Wembley signal control room. I've just asked them on the radio to look at this train, so if you would all like to show them exactly what you think of them, please go ahead. One or two fingers should be all you need.

> *Helpful advice from the driver of a London Underground train, on a stretch of line that was overground*

Don't go further on to be robbed. Step in here.

> *Notice in a boot-maker's shop window in the English Midlands. Advertisement recorded in* Bulls, Blunders and Howlers, *1928*

It's better to buy a $1 stock if it goes up 100 per cent, than to buy a $50 sock that will go up 100 per cent,

Jim Coleman, former assistant US attorney and partner of law firm
Ballard Spahr Andrews & Ingersol, Philadelphia

Not intended for highway use.

Warning notice on a 13-inch wheel on a garden wheelbarrow

This is a customer announcement. Would the nutter who just jumped onto the track please get back onto the platform as the rats get jealous when someone invades their territory.

Announcement by London Underground

Famous and Infamous Last Words

Die, my dear doctor? That's the last thing I shall do.

Lord Palmerston

Shoot Walter, in heaven's name!

Last words of the English King William II (1058–1100), who was out hunting with his friend Walter Tirel. During the hunt, Tirel fired an arrow at a stag. The arrow missed the animal and hit William Rufus in the chest. Within a few minutes the king was dead. Tirel jumped on his horse and made off at great speed. He escaped to France and quite wisely never returned to England

I'm bored, I'm bored.

Last words of Gabriele D'Annunzio, Italian poet

I am about to—or am I going to—die; either expression is used.

Last words of French grammarian and Jesuit priest Dominique Bouhours—a stickler for detail to the very last

I've never felt better.

> *Swashbuckling Hollywood hero Douglas Fairbanks' dying words*

Here lyes the Bodeys of George Young and Isobel Gutherie and all their
Posterity for more than fifty years backwards.

> *Epitaph on a tombstone, eighteenth century*

There's nothing about my life that is an accident.

> *Marc Bolan, of the Seventies rock band T-Rex,*
> *shortly before his fatal car crash*

Here lies Fuller's earth.

> *Epitaph of a certain Dr Fuller, who had requested that one of his companions*
> *write his epitaph for him—this was what he received*

My fun days are over.

> *Passing comment from James Dean, Hollywood actor,*
> *shortly before the car crash that killed him*

I can't sleep.

> *J.M. Barrie, British author and creator of* Peter Pan,
> *moments before he breathed his last*

I should never have switched from scotch to martinis.

> *Humphrey Bogart (d. 1957)*

Codeine . . . bourbon.

>> *Tallulah Bankhead when, as she was dying (in 1968), she was asked if there was*
any final thing she wanted

Are you sure it's safe?

>> *Last words of William Palmer, the infamous poisoner, while mounting*
the gallows from which he was to be hung

Only one man ever understood me. And he didn't understand me.

>> *Enigmatic last words of George Wilhelm Hegel, German philosopher*

The answer. What is the answer? . . . In that case, what is the question?

>> *Last words attributed to Gertrude Stein, American author,*
who was renowned for her enigmatic style of prose

Boys, boys, you wouldn't hang your sheriff, would you?

>> *Henry Plummer, sheriff of Bannock, Washington state, whose citizens finally*
rose up in protest against his strong-arm tactics, and did exactly that in 1864

Shakespeare, I come.

>> *Last words of Theodore Dreiser, American novelist (he had actually planned*
what to say in advance, as he admitted to H.L. Mencken, his friend)

Qualis artifex pereo!

>> *Last words of the Roman emperor Nero Claudius Caesar, who killed*
himself (translates as, "What an artist dies in me!")

Woe's me! I suppose I am becoming a God.

> *Last words of the Roman emperor Vespasian, according to Suetonius.*
> *(Those Roman emperors were nothing if not modest)*

It is nothing. It is nothing.

> *Last words of Archduke Ferdinand, after being shot in Sarajevo in 1914—the*
> *assassination proved to be the catalyst for the outbreak of World War I*

Like a worn-out type, he is returned to the founder, in hope of being re-cast in a
better and more perfect mould.

> *Nineteenth-century epitaph of a printer from Bury St Edmunds, East Anglia*

Hurrah, my boys! At the Parson's fall.
For if he'd liv'd longer he'd a-buried us alll.

> *Epitaph of local parson in South Wales*

Bugger Bognor.

> *Last words (allegedly) of the English King George V*

Here lies an editor.

> *Nineteenth-century epitaph*

One (goldfish) is bigger than the other two, and these latter are to be easily
recognized, as one is fat and the other lean.

> *Last will and testament of a woman who left seventy pounds a year for the*
> *upkeep of her three, beloved goldfish*

When I left England, I still couldn't go on the street . . . it took me years to unwind. I would be walking around tense like, waiting for somebody to say something or jump me. I can go right out of this door now and go in a restaurant. You want to know how great that is?

John Lennon, speaking in 1980. He was shot and killed by deranged fan Mark Chapman as he stepped out of his New York apartment onto the New York City sidewalk in December 1980

What an irreplaceable loss!

Last words of Auguste Comte, French philosopher

What's this?

Last words of Leonard Bernstein, American composer

Here lies the wife of Simon Stokes,
Who lived and died—like other folks.

Inscription on a tombstone

Here I lays,
Killed by a chaise.

Epitaph of a postilion

Lift me up that I may die standing, not lying down like a cow.

Last words of Siward, warrior Earl of Northumberland (c.1055)

What would they want with an old man like me?

> *Earl Mountbatten, brushing aside fears that he might become an IRA target in*
> *1978. He was killed in just such a terrorist attack the following year*

Why not? After all, it belongs to him.

> *Last words of Charlie Chaplin, upon being told,*
> *"May the Lord have mercy on your soul"*

Peas to his Hashes!

> *Epitaph of a London cook (the words playing on the phrase,*
> *"Peace to his ashes")*

Posterity will ne'er survey
A nobler grave than this:
Here lie the bones of Castlereagh
Stop, traveler, and piss.

> *Epitaph of Viscount Castlereagh (1769–1822)*

No . . . awfully jolly of you to suggest it, though.

> *Last words of Ronald Knox, English priest, when asked by his friend Lady Elton*
> *if he wished to hear her read from his own translation of the New Testament*

I think we just sort of grew out of drugs. The drugs aren't necessary now.

> *Keith Moon of the rock band The Who, in 1977. He died of a drug*
> *and alcohol overdose in September 1978*

Underneath this pile of stones

Lies all that's left of Sally Jones

Her name was Lord, it was not Jones

But Jones was used to rhyme with stones.

Epitaph in Skaneateles, New York

Dorothy Cecil, unmarried as yet.

Epitaph on a tomb in Wimbledon, South London

It's been a long time since I've had champagne.

Last words of the Russian playwright Anton Chekhov

Thank you, sister. May you be the mother of a bishop!

Irish playwright Brendan Behan's words to the nun who was

nursing him on his deathbed

Here lies my wife Polly, a terrible shrew,

If I said I was sorry, I should lie too.

Epitaph in an Australian graveyard

Thomas Thomson's buried here,

And what is more, he's in his bier.

In life, thy beer did thee surround,

And now with thee is in the ground.

Epitaph of a publican

Here lies my wife, a slattern and shrew:
If I said I regretted her, I should lie too.

Epitaph in Selby, Yorkshire

I hate to say it, but crime is an overhead you have to pay if you want to live in
this city.

George Moscone, then Mayor of San Francisco, interviewed by Newsweek
*magazine in December 1976. He was later shot dead by a former policeman
with a serious grudge to bear*

He that dyed so oft in sport
Dyed at last, no color for't.

Epitaph on a dyer

Here lies—
Who came to this city and died
For the benefit of his health.

Epitaph in a cemetery near Cincinnati

Goodbye . . . if you hear of my being stood up against a Mexican stone wall and
shot to rags please know that I think that a pretty good way to depart this
life. It beats old age, disease, or falling down the cellar stairs. To be a Gringo
in Mexico—ah, that is euthanasia!

Last known words of Ambrose Bierce (author of The Devil's Dictionary*),
in a farewell letter to his niece, Lora. Brose quit the US in 1913, aged 71, to
observe the Pancho Villa revolution in Mexico*

So who's in a hurry?

>> *Robert Benchley, American author, when warned that he was slowly drinking*
>> *himself to death*

Wait till I have finished my problem!

>> *Last words of Archimedes, Greek mathematician (his dying phrases have also*
>> *been recorded as 'Stand away, fellow, from my diagram', and*
>> *"Don't disturb my circles!" respectively)*

Here lies the body of John Day:
What, young John? No, no. Old John? Aye.

>> *Epitaph on a tombstone*

Here lies W. W.
Who never more will trouble you trouble you.

>> *Epitaph on one "W. W."*

Am I dying or is it my birthday?

>> *Last words of Nancy, Lady Astor, upon seeing her entire family*
>> *gathered around her sick bed*

Here lies the body of Thomas Parr,
What, Old Tom? No! What, Young Tom? Ah!

>> *Epitaph in Swaffham churchyard, Norfolk*

I don't need bodyguards.

> *Comment by Jimmy Hoffa, labor leader, in a* Playboy *interview,*
> *December 1975 – he subsequently went missing (presumed dead)*

His life and death five letters do express—
A B C he knew not, and died of X S.

> *Epitaph "of a Sot"*

Waiting, are they? Waiting, are they? Well—let 'em wait!

> *Last words of Ethan Allen, hero of the American Revolution, on being told by*
> *his doctor, "General, I fear the angels are waiting for you"*

I do not have to forgive my enemies; I have had them all shot.

> *Last words of Ramon Maria Narvaez, eighteenth-century*
> *Spanish general and politician*

Here lies a man,
Misform'd and misshapen,
His name it was
John Wood Capon

> *Epitaph of John Woodcock—his name was changed so that it would*
> *rhyme with "misshapen"*

Don't worry, it's not loaded.

> *Terry Kath, of the pop group Chicago, demonstrating a revolver*
> *to the other members of the band in 1978*

Acknowledgments

The author would like to thank the ever-helpful staff at the London Library and also at the British Library, where much of this book was researched and written.

A small proportion of the quotes featured between these covers have appeared in a number of anthologies, or else have whizzed around the world on the Internet a couple of times before being spotted, often with minor variations of punctuation and/or grammar. On such rare occasions, it's proved difficult in the extreme both to verify the precise wording of the original quotation and the first recorder of it. In these instances, the quotes were just too good to miss out, so have been included. My thanks to whoever it was that first jotted down these particular *bons mots*–and apologies to any other author who might feel that I have trodden on their toes.